The Sound of the Dolphin's Psalm

Libby Layne

The Sound of the Dolphin's Psalm

Library of Congress Catalog Card Number
97-60211

ISBN: 1-890306-01-0

Warwick House

Publishing

720 Court Street
Lynchburg, Virginia

Let every creature rise and bring
Peculiar honors to our King
Angels descend with songs again
And earth repeat the loud Amen
Isaac Watts

To Our Creator

I Dedicate This

My Peculiar Honor

ACKNOWLEDGMENTS

Until Molly Roper Jenkins became involved in this project, I had only a vague idea of the function of an editor. I imagined someone who would correct punctuation and grammar and perhaps rearrange a few paragraphs here and there. Most certainly she did teach me how to use "its" and "it's" correctly, to put quotations outside the punctuation, and proper use of commas, colons and semicolons. Little did I know she would become part of the soul of my book. She immediately perceived the essence of my story from one reading of a rough, disorganized first draft and believed it could be a book. From that point she was my constant guide in reconstructing the pieces of my puzzle into a meaningful whole. She encouraged my belief both in the value of the story and my ability to write it well. Most importantly, she cared enough about its message not to allow our friendship to interfere with her critical and superior editing skills. For her talent, her support, and her "essence" I am profoundly grateful.

As I neared publication, my sister Barbara Melby and Joyce Maddox of Warwick House were there to fine-tune the final manuscript. I thank them for their honest and vital input, as well as their excitement on reading my story. They gave me additional confidence that writing it had been a good idea.

To the parents of the children in my DOLFA-WAVE study, I owe a great debt. I am grateful for their initial willingness to let me work with their children and in now allowing me to use their stories as part of my own story. I have been blessed by their presence in my life.

Thanks also:

To my Dad, a "pseudo-agnostic," who from my childhood challenged my beliefs, forcing me to sort them out for myself; who teased me about my peculiarities and eccentricities which in the end became fertile ground for my wonderful adventure; whose love I never doubted; and who is, today, quite proud of his strange little girl.

To my mother, whose poetic spirit I must have inherited; who lived, joyfully, the premise that being wife and mother is a wonderful career; who, after the age of fifty, published a book of poetry, started a craft business in a vacated chicken house, and painted portraits for governors; who showed me that being a woman is not limited by our society, only by ourselves.

Finally, to my husband, Harry, I am especially grateful. If it were not for his attitude toward my journey, I would never have had it. He encouraged the freedom I have felt for thirty-five years to follow my rather unusual interests and passions. His constant reminder that I not "blow out my own candle" has served as an underpinning for my explorations and adventures. And best of all, the candle we have kept lit together burns ever brighter as the years go by.

PROGRAMME

I
Overture

*Everything in the Universe is subject to change
and everything is right on schedule.*
(anonymous)

What is Truth, then?
(Pilate, *The Passion According to John,* J.S. Bach)

Everything in this book may not be true.
(*Illusions,* Richard Bach)

Truth is not a belief.

The stories haunt me, transporting my imagination to beaches I've never walked, yet remember vividly. They introduce me to women I've never met, yet know intimately. They speak a truth that touches me at the deepest level of my being, yet ...

The small, green, paperback jumped off the shelf in the book store screaming, "Buy *me,* buy *me!*"

The penetrating green eyes of the old woman on the cover stare out from an understated black and white sketch, beckoning me to enter her world. Inhabiting this world are people of an ancient culture, remnants of which still live on an island near the coast of Vancouver, British Columbia.

The stories revolve around a society of women, descendants of Copper Woman, the first human in the Nootka culture's creation myth. According to this myth, all the peoples of the earth — black, white, yellow and red — also descended from Copper Woman and were dispersed throughout the world by a Great Flood. There are stories of the coming of the white man, bringing with him not only his religion, but corruption and disease which decimated the Indian population.

Special women in this culture had preserved these stories and myths orally for generations, from as far back as time. From mother to daughter, grandmother to granddaughter, aunt to niece, they were passed along like precious pearls, until finally they were shared with the author of the little green book I now held in my hand. She had been given permission by the women, in what ultimately became a secret society, to write the stories; the pearls were in danger of being forever lost to a modern society.

I am enchanted by the simple beauty of these myths and, at the same time, astounded at the depth of the profound truths I find hidden within them. I am mystified by the connection I feel to this culture, as if reviving a long-lost memory. Whatever the connection, after reading the book again and again, I feel compelled to find these women.

Harry and I are planning a month-long motorhome trip to the Northwest, providing a perfect opportunity to find the women and hear the stories firsthand.

We share an interest in Native American cultures and visit several as we camp our way across the country. There are many roadside vendors, selling their native crafts from battered pick-up trucks and makeshift booths. At one such "store," I meet a lovely young Navaho woman selling beaded jewelry she has made. After making a purchase, I tell her of my quest and ask, "Have you ever heard the stories of Copper Woman?"

"Oh yes, my grandfather has been telling me those stories since I was a little girl. He thought it was so important that he took us up there. It feels different, I can't explain it."

We talk more of the women, the stories, and as I walk to the car she calls to me, "Have a good trip." Then almost as an afterthought, "Keep an open heart."

I felt it was a blessing of some kind. I was definitely on the right path in my quest.

With more than three thousand miles behind us, we finally turn north toward the US/Canadian border. Harry has agreed to help find my mythical island, though I have scant knowledge of where it is or how to get there. Nearing Vancouver, I scan my book once again for any clue to the island's location. The information had been there all along, hiding in the acknowledgments section. How had I missed it until now?

The women of the stories live on Ahousat Island off the coast of Vancouver Island. It is not, however, on any map in our possession. Undaunted, I am positive that when we get to Canada, everyone will know about the myths and will tell me exactly where to go. Certainly these wonderful stories are common knowledge among the people there, particularly the Nootka Indians about whom the stories are told.

Reading a visitor's guide picked up on the ferry to Vancouver Island, I find confirmation, at last, that the Island of Ahousat exists outside my book. It is pictured as a tourist attraction where one might go to observe a native culture and shop in a village store for handmade crafts. I am greatly relieved to learn that not only does the island exist, but it is advertised as a safe place to visit. A small map locates the island several miles off the west coast of the fishing village of Torino. Our extensive campsite book lists only two campgrounds on the entire West Coast of Vancouver Island; neither takes reservations. This could be a problem. No matter; problems can be solved. Armed with my eternal optimism, we forge ahead in our twenty-eight-foot motorhome.

As Harry drives, I watch the open, spacious highway become a winding mountain road. Snow-capped peaks and clear, silver-blue lakes appear on either side as we creep carefully upward. The mountain road becomes more and more narrow, as hairpin curves carry us higher into a misty cloud cover. At one juncture, in order to negotiate a curve, the RV must be maneuvered back and forth as though we are squeezing into a tight parallel parking spot. Throughout this entire ordeal, Harry keeps his humor, never complaining. After almost thirty years of marriage, I found myself falling in love with him all over again. We were on a wild goose chase to an unknown destination for a hair-brained reason he didn't understand, and on he drove!

Leaving the mountains behind us, we relax as the road becomes more RV-friendly and evidence of civilization reappears. Signs direct us to the first campground on our list. There is no vacancy. The same is true of the second, but the owner will allow us to stay the night in the parking lot. Tomorrow morning a beautiful site will be available right on the ocean. We walk to the site through the lush, green Canadian Rain Forest. What I see takes my breath away.

A thick, heavy mist hangs over everything, giving the scene an eerie, mystical appearance. Huge boulders jut up out of the surf - like massive sentinels waiting for the crash of oncoming waves. The beach is covered with large pieces of greying driftwood and thousands of mollusk shells. I feel a strong sense of familiarity. More than a remembrance of the description in the book, I feel as if I have been here.

Since the proprietor of the campground has lived here most of his life, I inquire about Ahousat Island, "Do you know the legend of Copper Woman and the Nootka women on Ahousat Island who tell the stories of her?"

"Never heard anything about the stories, but I've been to Ahousat. In Torino you can arrange to go there by boat or seaplane. No problem."

We walk the short distance into Torino, a small fishing village where I begin to see signs of the native population. I ask people I meet about the legend of Copper Woman and the women's society; I receive only blank expressions.

"Never heard of it," they say.

As I repeat my question again and again, receiving the same answer, I begin to feel a bit silly. I continue on to the seaplane office, however, where I ask about going to Ahousat. The clerk says it is quite safe, though I probably won't find anyone there but Nootkas. They have a flight leaving tomorrow at 1:00 PM.

"The fare is usually $75.00 a person, but since our pilot is taking some other folks over that way tomorrow, we'll charge you half."

"This is encouraging," I say to myself, relieved that I know the Nootka women I have come to visit actually live on the island.

I have already informed Harry that he is not invited on my quest; this is something I must do alone. Though he is uneasy about my flying off in a seaplane to an unknown island, he never tries to convince me otherwise. He knows of my determination and has been assured by the townspeople that I will be safe.

The next day, carrying both a copy of the book about Copper

Woman and high expectations, I go to the dock where the seaplane floats awkwardly in the water. Walking toward the plane on the wooden pier, I ask a native-looking woman about the stories.

"I never heard of them," is her now-familiar reply.

Doubts about the wisdom of my pilgrimage are beginning to surface, but I've come this far and it's too late to turn back now. I agree to call Harry from Ahousat if I will be returning later than 3:00 PM.

I board the seaplane and sit beside a Caucasian woman traveling with two native children; she says she is married to a Nootka man.

"Aha," I think, "she'll know something."

"Never heard of that," is the all too-familiar reply.

The propellers begin to spin, the motors sputter, the plane taxies across the water and lifts off into the misty sky. "What in the *world* are you *doing?*" I say to myself.

Here I am flying to a native island where there are only Nootka Indians, and I don't know a soul. Not to mention the fact that I am beginning to wonder whether the stories of Copper Woman exist outside my little green book.

The noisy plane reaches a flying altitude not far above the water, and I see the beaches of Vancouver Island pass below me. I peer out of the clouded window wondering which of these garden paradises is the one I seek; to which beach did Copper Woman first come?

After only fifteen minutes, we land in shallow water by a decaying wooden dock. I cautiously crawl out of the plane onto the dock which stretches to the beach of Ahousat Island. I watch as the seaplane takes off across the water, disappearing into the distance, leaving me standing alone on a remote island with my book of Copper Woman and a quest that is beginning to feel ridiculous.

The island looks almost deserted. There is *nothing* to suggest that any tourist would be welcome here. There is no store, there are no crafts, there are no friendly Nootkas waiting to give me a tour of the island. Ramshackle houses and empty buildings dot the path winding up to the main village. There are a few half-naked children playing and some mangy dogs fighting over a meal in a rotting garbage heap.

I walk up to a house that looks inhabited and knock on the door. The windows are open and I hear sounds from inside; I assume there is someone home. I continue knocking until a woman appears at the upstairs window. She is not happy to see me and frowns as I launch into the story of my purpose for being here.

No, she has never heard of a secret society. No, she never heard of Copper Woman or the myths and stories about the island.

"Is there *anyone* who might know?" I ask.

Begrudgingly, she points up the street, "An elder of the tribe lives up there. He might know." My confidence crumbling, I trudge up the hill to a white frame house whose condition is only slightly superior to others around it. In the front yard is an ancient Cadillac being repaired by an even more ancient native man.

"I am from Virginia in the USA. I have come three thousand miles to find the women who tell the stories of Copper Woman and this island. Do you know anything about this?"

I hold up the book with the piercing green eyes of Copper Woman staring out. He looks at me, looks at the book, then back at me.

"BULL SHIT!"

Taken aback, I say, "Excuse me?"

"Bull Shit, that's all it is. She made it all up. You cut me to the quick when you mention that lady's name. Terrible, evil woman. Spoke lies."

"So the stories are not true?"

"All lies," he states, matter-of-factly. I suddenly recall a passage in the book in which the young woman, who is finally given permission to write down the stories after centuries of oral tradition asks, "What will people say, what will the men say?"

The wise old woman answers, "They'll say it's Bull Shit." Finally I have something to go on! This Nootka man has reacted exactly as predicted in the Copper Woman book and has used, verbatim, the same expletive. My confidence is restored; I now have fresh fuel for my mission.

"Are there any women in the house with whom I can speak?"

"Yes," he says, giving me permission to go in, "my wife and some others."

"At last," I think excitedly, "I will sit at the feet of the Nootka women, listening to the ancient myths and stories of Copper Woman. They will be astonished at the long journey I have made just to meet them. My deep understanding of the stories will so touch them that I will be inducted as an honorary member of the secret society of women. And then, at last, I will be presented my official headband of trade-beads tied on a black cord in a simple, but elegant, ancient ceremony."

Heart beating wildly, I knock on the door. It is opened by a young native woman, and I peer into a rather darkened room. On an over-stuffed sofa is seated an old Nootka woman I assume is the elder's wife. There are several other younger women and two or three native children. All look at me curiously as if to say, "Why is there a white woman standing in our doorway?" On the far wall is a large picture of a fair-skinned, blue-eyed Jesus, with long blond hair and beard; one like it hung in my Sunday School class as a child. The room is cluttered with well-used furniture, and there is a Merry Christmas sign with red and white tinsel around it hanging askew on another wall. I am invited in, and though they must be astounded at my presence there, they are calm and courteous. I feel no fear.

I tell them the purpose of my visit.

"I am looking for the women who tell the stories of Copper Woman," I repeat, hoping to see *any* positive response from *anyone*. "I have read this book about the legends and stories."

I am met with blank expressions and no response.

"All I want to know is if the stories are true," I plead, now at the brink of tears.

The ancient old woman sits quietly listening to my tale. Her copper-toned face is deeply wrinkled and the wisdom of the ages is written in her eyes. She suddenly speaks in English intermixed with Nootka, "Yes, it's true."

Hearing those words finally spoken, I burst into tears, releasing a flood of frustration built up in the past twenty-four hours. As we continue to talk, however, I realize she has misunderstood. The other women explain she had thought I was speaking of a book her husband had written about the island. Again, they deny any knowledge of Copper Woman, her stories and the society of women.

I sob now in disappointment as they quietly sit and watch, not seeming uncomfortable with my outburst.

"May we see the book?"

They look at the dedication, nodding as they recognize several of the names.

"We know Mary and Margaret used to live here."

"Yes, we remember something about a woman coming here to get information for a movie a few years ago, but we never heard of Copper Woman or the stories."

The old woman speaks again.

"All lies," she says flatly.

"You are telling me that there was no secret society, no legend of Copper Woman? You are saying the author came here and invented the stories to sell books?"

"I suppose so."

The old woman then brings out a copy of the history of Ahousat, written by her husband. "*This* is the truth."

Finally composed, I begin to laugh at the scene I had created here. I had traveled three thousand miles across the United States, trekked over treacherous mountains in a large RV, and had flown in a seaplane to a remote island, only to learn that the stories I believed carried great truths were nothing but a fabrication of an inventive author! The women sit, listening quietly as I muse over the implications of my misguided journey.

"These stories touched me so deeply. It was as if I had lived them myself. They were stories of strong, capable, loving and highly spiritual women. They were the kind of women I would like to be," I declare, as much to myself as to them.

I suddenly come to a realization.

"It makes no difference if someone invented the stories, they speak *truth* to me!" I say confidently.

They only smile.

"May I go back to the main island right away?"

"The boat leaves in five minutes," replies one young woman, "I'll call and ask them to wait for you." I thank them, buy the book written by the old woman's husband and notice that the young woman is staying on the phone for quite awhile. The women appear to be touched by my situation. The old man, whom I have learned is a respected leader or elder of the tribe, enters the room from outside.

"She said that our women wore nothing on the top. That's a lie." He literally spat the words.

I leave the house, walking down to the boat, thinking, "What a hoot. I came all this way to find out some opportunist woman author had made up some myths, passing them off as truth, and I swallowed it hook, line and sinker."

I shrug it off and chalk it up to a crazy, wonderful adventure.

As I board the boat, I am laughing at myself. When the young Nootka man who pilots the boat asks why, I tell him my story.

"Let me see the book."

He leafs through it, looks at the dedication, then nods his head. "This woman is my grandmother and this one is my wife's grandmother." He pauses, waiting for me to speak.

"Are you saying the stories are true?" I ask, almost afraid of the answer.

"Oh, yes, they are true."

I show him the headband I had made like the ones described in the book. "Have you ever seen one of these?"

"Yes, my grandmother would have worn one of those."

"But where are the women who tell the stories?"

"Either dead or moved to the city."

I explain what I had experienced on Ahousat.

"Well, you know, people forget," he says quietly.

I didn't ask why the women in the house had not told me. I already knew. Those women were like the women later in the book, after the men's culture began to dominate what had been a beautiful culture of men and women working together as equals. Neither gender was suppressed or diminished in any way. The elder who had said, "Bull Shit," was merely taking his place in the patriarchal system established by the Catholic missionaries in more recent history. The women told me nothing because the secret society had to be kept secret, even now, in that home.

I pieced together what must have happened. The young woman who phoned was probably related in some way to the young man on the boat. In her call to him, she made certain that before I left the island, I would know the stories of Copper Woman and the society of women were based on fact; they were true. For this I am forever grateful to her.

Before I was allowed this information, however, I realized it was necessary that I come to a place of complete confidence in my own sense of the truth — even when everything I was experiencing pointed otherwise.

Is there Truth with a capital T? Is there one underlying Truth that would unite our varied belief systems, yet allow us the freedom for individual interpretation? Is there Truth that would satisfy our longing for the mystical, the miraculous, and at the same time meet our insistence on scientific reason?

Einstein searched until his death for a theory in physics which would combine inclusively his separate hypotheses of electromagnetism, gravitation and relativity. He tentatively called this a "Unified Field Theory." Is there a *spiritual* Unified Field? Might they be one and the same? Does this kind of Truth exist, or are we doomed to a pilgrimage of half-believed creeds, antiquated doctrines and divisive dogmas? Saying, "There is no Truth with a capital T," perhaps you have given up your search altogether.

My own search urges me ever forward in the belief that there is such Truth. Though elusive, I know, somehow, that it exists. Its teachers come to all cultures and religions. They appear in every age and are many times not easily recognizable bearers of the sacred. Such were the teachers who illuminated my life's journey. Subtly they entered my world, giving no clue of the mysteries they would reveal or how they would become inextricably connected.

Early in my journey, I was unaware of any teaching from, or purpose to, the teacher forms being introduced to me willy-nilly. Even after I recognized the significance of the forms themselves, the connections between them were obscure. It was as if all the pieces of a puzzle had been placed on the table, but someone had misplaced the box top showing the total picture. I could either spend my time looking for the box top or simply move ahead, working the puzzle as the picture developed. In choosing the latter, my life became an adventure. My teacher forms were sent to teach Truth in ways I could best understand it. The shapes they took varied from delicate to grotesque, graceful to clumsy, playful to inactive, melodic to dissonant, brilliant to retarded. Each had a unique and exceptional way of communicating, and each demanded the challenge that I learn this communication — that I enter *their* world on *their* terms.

It was only after I had written the first draft of my story that I discovered yet another teacher who had been with me "unawares" throughout.

There is, of course, a certain risk in the presumption that what I perceive as Truth is of any consequence to anyone else, or that my story is worth telling. To the end that it encourages others on their inward journey, I will venture on. Though it is but one individual's quest for answers, I sense that at the very heart of things is a Universal Truth that transcends every barrier we human creatures have erected between each other, between ourselves and the rest of creation. It is for this Truth we must all search, each in our own way.

It is this Truth that will set us free.

To seek
is as good as seeing

God wants us
to search earnestly
and with perseverance
without sloth
and worthless sorrow

We must know
that God will appear suddenly
and joyfully
to all lovers of God

Julian of Norwich

II
Introit

> *"Be not forgetful to entertain strangers;*
> *for thereby some have entertained angels unawares."*
> Hebrews 13:1-2

Sometimes it is hard to know when a story begins, especially one you have been part of for forever or more. One of the mysteries of being an angel is how we view this thing you call time. It is almost impossible to explain to human beings that in eternity there are no minutes, days, months or years as you know them. Only as we take human form on earth is life so marked.

My name is Robin Elizabeth. I was born with what is now called Down's Syndrome, though people in those days called us "Mongoloid" because of our slanty eyes. Very little was known about us, and even good doctors knew no better than to suggest we be put away in institutions for the rest of our lives. My parents decided, instead, to take me home and love me just as I was.

I was in earthly form for two years, your time. It was a short time by human measure, but long enough to do what I was sent to do. After I left earth and came back here, my mother wrote a book about me and the impact I made on their lives. Many people since then have been touched by reading this book; their lives have been forever changed. This is the story about one of those people; her name is Elizabeth, too.

She will tell her own story, the part she knows and has come to understand. I will be helping her tell it, though she will be unaware of this, as she has been unaware of my guiding presence throughout her life. In this way, I may also help you understand how life can be seen as a wonderful and mysterious puzzle. As she works her puzzle, sorting and fitting each of the many pieces, you may find clues to your own life's puzzle. Though each puzzle is entirely different, each life story unique, all are connected in some way.

At one time she thought of her story only as an adventure. But lately — lately she has begun to hear
The Sound of the Dolphin's Psalm

The Mystery

Because the dolphin lives perfectly within creation,
His LIFE is a Psalm.
As we learn to live perfectly within creation,
Our LIFE will also be a PSALM,
A Psalm of Praise and Thanksgiving to the Creator
Whose Love
Solves the Mystery of
The Sound of the Dolphin's Psalm.

Present Day

Has it really been almost thirty years since those wonderful creatures invaded my life? They certainly have been the common denominator of my journey for those years. Though I am positive they in themselves are not the Truth, perhaps they hold clues to the mystery I wish to solve.

My search for clues begins as I rummage through file after file of information I have collected relating to the dolphins. I reread every personal note I've written in my journals that applies to them. I look at each photograph taken on my yearly dolphin swims. I watch videos taken of me swimming in the clear waters of the Bahamas, weaving in and out of a pod of Atlantic Spotteds. I see an enlarged photo on my wall, which I took, of a dolphin's eye looking directly into my own. With each memory I resurrect, I am overcome with awe and gratitude for what I have been allowed to experience.

As I search through my dolphin memorabilia, I notice that one of my dream journals has somehow found its way into the cardboard box. I don't remember putting it there. Curious, I pick it up and it falls open to a page on which I recorded a dream I had entitled, "The secret of sound and healing." In this dream I am told there is someone who can reveal the secret of the healing power of sound. The one who holds the secret is French! The remainder of the dream is rather bizarre and doesn't relate to anything in particular, but what leaps out at me is this *Frenchman* who knows the secret. Suddenly I feel the hairs on the back of my neck stand on end; my heart begins to race. There is a connection here, I know it! Could this be the vital clue for which I have been searching? After all these years, might the mystery of the *Sound of the Dolphin's Psalm* be solved? Might the pieces of this amazing puzzle at last come together into a meaningful picture?

I note the date of the dream; it is 1989. This was *before* I met Betsy Smith, *before* Dolphinswim, *before* DOLFA-WAVE and *before* my first swim with the research group. Most importantly, it was *before* I discovered Alfred Tomatis, the *French* ENT physician, whose work had led to a treatment used with autistic individuals! How incredible that the information appeared in my dreams before that piece of the puzzle was made available to me. Even more intriguing is the fact that it had surfaced at this moment, as I struggle to make some sense of my extraordinary journey.

Almost afraid to look, I go to my bookshelf and take down Alfred Tomatis's autobiography, *The Conscious Ear*. Throughout the book I had highlighted certain passages that applied to my research with the autistic children and the dolphin sounds. Several years before my study, I had read these passages, sensing something significant there. At the time, however, the significance was hidden from me — it was too soon to make the final connection. Now, as I excitedly reread the information, I know that the time has come. The final clue lies waiting for me here. Hardly breathing, I turn the page...

"You are almost there," my Spirit tells me. "You are almost there!"

III
Theme

Thursday, April 18, 1996

I'm obsessing again! Each year before a dolphin swim trip, I enact this same ritual, checking and rechecking the day and date on my plane reservation. The timing is critical. To board the *Sea Fever*, sailing early Saturday morning, I must arrive Friday afternoon and spend the night in a hotel near the marina.

I look at the departure time again. The ticket says Friday, 9:35 AM, the boarding pass and latest itinerary say 9:15. I wonder which one is correct; probably the latter. It's a good thing I checked. I would have missed my plane.

In January, when we left home for three months, I hid my ticket, assuring its safety until I returned. After the trip, I searched for days in all my favorite hiding places before finding it... in our motor home. As an extra precaution, I had taken the ticket with me in the event our house burned to the ground while we were gone!

Inspection of my luggage, which I began packing weeks ago, is next. Methodically, I compare each item with my list: three bathing suits, three towels, my collection of dolphin T-shirts, shorts, underwear, sunblock, toiletries, wet suit, flippers, mask and snorkel, camera and film. I scan my medicine packet: Benadryl for the sea lice, swimmers ear stuff, vitamins, decongestant, aspirin, and seasick medicine. Do I have enough Bonine? I couldn't get the scopolomine patch this year; something about the factory closing in Mexico.

I make visual contact with my passport, noticing it expires February, 1997. Has it really been ten years since I first got it? I must make a note to get a new one before next year's swim.

There are good-bye calls to family — children, sisters, and parents. Mom always worries that either the sharks or the Bermuda Triangle will get me. There are casseroles in the refrigerator for Harry, dog food for Moe, and bird seed for the birds. Did I forget anything?

After we go out to dinner tonight, I'll rent a boring movie. With any luck, it will make me drowsy and I can get to sleep. The mere thought of the next two weeks causes smiles, tears, and butterflies simultaneously. After five years of this same routine, you might expect I'd be calmer. Instead, like a kid at Christmas, I babble to everyone I meet, "Tomorrow I leave to swim with wild dolphins in the Bahama Banks!"

Friday, April 19, 1996

Morning has finally come, following a night of waking every hour to look at the clock. (There is always the possibility my alarm won't go off.) I check my departure time just *once* more before eating a light breakfast. I cram last-minute items into my two huge carry-ons, which I will lug through airports. This is a precaution against any checked luggage getting lost. There is no margin for error here. We board the *Sea Fever* at 8:00 AM tomorrow and there is no way to retrieve essential diving equipment once out to sea.

Obsessing again, I check my belly-bag for passport, travelers checks, Visa card and airline ticket. Then we're off to the airport for a 9:15 departure. (I'm *sure* it's 9:15)

"Are you excited?" a silly question, Harry knows, but asks anyway. This is one trip we don't take together; he calls it his "two weeks off."

I go to the airline counter where my ticket is checked against the agent's computer. My anxiety mounts as he punches numbers into a machine I still don't trust. What if someone hit the wrong key and my reservation is floating somewhere in cyberspace? After all, I made it six months ago! As I see the agent mark my ticket, signifying everything is in order, I relax.

"Are you checking your bags?"

Struggling to make them appear smaller and lighter than they really are, I lift them up for him to see.

"No thanks," I say cheerily, praying he won't ask me to measure them in the little measuring box.

Downstairs at the departure gates, friends and neighbors wait for flights to weddings or business trips. Welcoming any opportunity to go on and on about my exciting destination, I hope someone will ask where *I'm* going.

The familiar faces at this end of my trip remind me that at the other end I will know no one except Rebecca and Captain Tom. Each year a new group gathers from all over the world to spend the week at sea with the dolphins and each other.

I board the plane as the engines begin to warm up. I recite a little mantra to my airplane angels — "Angels surround us, angels protect us and bring us safely to our journey's end."

Suddenly, the speaker crackles. "Ladies and gentlemen, this is the captain speaking," the man says in one of those calm, captain-like voices that immediately makes you suspicious.

"Our number two engine doesn't seem to want to start. Would all of the passengers please deplane while we get maintenance to take a look? Sorry for the inconvenience."

Well, *this* has never happened to me before. Is this an omen of some kind or just a practical time problem in making connections?

As we get off the plane we are requested to make new reservations at the desk. Inside the terminal, people checking in for the 9:50 flight to Pittsburgh are asked to wait, in the event some of us need that connection. Most everyone is taking the situation in stride, agreeing it's best to discover the problem with Engine Number Two while still on the ground.

After waiting in line, I am finally re-booked — Lynchburg to Pittsburgh, Pittsburgh to Miami, Miami to Freeport instead of Lynchburg–Charlotte–Ft.Lauderdale–Freeport. The moment my new route is entered into the computer, the maintenance person runs in announcing, "The Charlotte 9:15 is ready to go." Back to plan "A."

A bit wary, I trudge back to the plane. We are now minus about half the original passengers who have rebooked and left the airport. Requesting that my airplane angels check to make certain Engine Number Two is *really* O.K., I'm off to Charlotte. My connection in Charlotte leaves at 11:15. *This* flight takes an hour, which is cutting it close; it is already 10:00. I repeatedly ask the attendant if they've called ahead to hold my flight. He smiles and nods, not as confidently as I'd like. At least I'm heading *south* instead of *north* to Pittsburgh!

I recline my seat and finally relax, suspended in time and space between my upcoming adventure and the path which has brought me here. I wonder when it *really* began.

Of course, even I don't know exactly when it began. Where I am there is only eternity, undivided into past, present or future. I do remember, though, the first time she met me. She was twelve years old, listening as her mother read the book my mother had written about me. In the years after our first meeting her life became an adventure.

To sustain her on this adventure she was given three wonderful gifts. The first was her love of, and talent for, music. The second, was a compassion for special children like me. The third gift was a strong determination to find meaning in everything in her life. This "spirit of tenacity" would be the most important gift of all, for it would guide her to her special teachers and urge her to learn from them certain truths about Creation and her place in it.

Her parents named her Elizabeth Layne, only that's not what everyone called her when she was little; they called her "Libby Layne." She had blond curly hair and blue eyes like mine and came into a family who loved her very much —just like mine...

"Praise Him, Praise Him, All Ye Little Children"

1940-1968

I began singing before I could talk and by the age of two years I knew more than twenty songs. As the first child of my parents and the second grandchild of my father's large family, this talent for music afforded me abundant and welcome adoration. Very early on, I became a willing performer and a consummate "ham." Mother and Daddy taught me all the usual children's nursery songs. In addition, my repertoire was greatly expanded by singing in Sunday School, in children's choir at church, and church services. It was singing these songs about the beautiful earth and all its creatures that first gave me a sense of who God is.

I never doubted there was a God interested in everything I did and was. I went to Sunday School and church where my family had gone for generations — the Church of the Brethren. I disliked preachers who angrily roared their sermons, pounding their fists on the pulpit for emphasis. I wondered if it hurt God's ears as it did mine and if He became as bored with their endlessly long prayers. On the other hand, I loved singing the hymns and listening to the stories. I always placed myself strategically behind a family and a baby with whom I could flirt when I became bored with the service. I was most uncomfortable when missionaries came as guests and chose to call people with whom they worked "heathens" because they believed differently about God.

I memorized every Bible story told me, from Noah's Flood to little Zacchaeus, who climbed the tree to see Jesus. I particularly identified with this one, as I was quite short. My favorites were ones in which Jesus scolded the grown-ups, telling them how important it was to love and be like little children.

One thing confused me most. Why would a minister say in

one breath that God loved everybody, and then, in the next, state they would go to hell if they weren't "saved"? That God, who loved everyone, would condemn anyone to a horrible place for eternity made no sense to me — and from just *what* were these people being "saved"? I had already begun searching for answers and wasn't afraid to ask my astonished Sunday School teachers my heretical questions. I seem to have been born with this relentless pursuit of the truth.

There was something else I sensed from the beginning: I had a purpose on earth and looking for that purpose was vitally important. I faithfully said my prayers and never once doubted that Someone heard them. I was always asking, "Why am I here?" My concern was that God would "call" me to be a missionary in Africa, and I knew I didn't want to do that *at all,* not wanting to be like the glum-faced missionaries I heard in church. But if God "called" you, you *had* to go, right? I would *have* to say, "Here I am, send me."

She really started asking important questions very early, didn't she? This is going to be quite a journey!

Almost twenty of your years have passed since I met Libby Layne, who is now called "Libby" by all but her family and me.

I have shared the joy of these twenty years as she became a woman, fell in love, married and had two children. As she grew and developed, so did her love and enjoyment of music, her first special gift. Music was an important part of her high school and college days, and since she married, she has continued to sing in community choruses, musical theater and in church choirs. She has also become active in community and church activities. Most of all she has enjoyed being a "stay-at-home" mother, satisfied this is the career for which she always prepared.

There is a war going on now in a place called Viet Nam, and Harry must serve two years in the Navy. Because he is needed to deliver babies, he is stationed at a U.S.-based Naval Hospital in Millington, Tennessee.

Here, Libby Layne is guided to some of her Very Special Teachers. I am near to make sure she recognizes them. She still doesn't recognize me.

July, 1969

As Harry and I arrive in Millington, Tennessee, I am *very* ready to deliver our third child. I loved being pregnant the first time, tolerated it the second, and am impatient to have the third over and done. We have left the other two children in Virginia with my mother until we find a place to live.

We are both excited as it is the first time either of us has lived outside "The Commonwealth." Our expectations are high as we explore our new town. After living in apartments all our married life, we are hoping to find a house to rent. We ask where we might buy a newspaper with classified ads.

"Let's see," drawls a young woman at the only drug store in town. "It's Thursday, yes, the weekly paper comes out today, you're in luck."

After searching the *one* page classified, we decide to take in a movie at the *one* local movie house. We walk into the darkened theater and sit down, the only persons there.

Somewhere in the theater we hear, "O.K. Billy, start the machine."

There is a click and a whirr as Billy starts the machine, and the movie, a Peter Sellers comedy, begins. Several times during the showing, Billy has trouble with the film breaking. By this time, we are in stitches, and not just from *The Pink Panther.* Our new adventure into the big wide world is more like a step backward in time.

We soon learn that renting a house will be expensive and too far from the hospital. As a last resort, we check into base housing.

"Yes, we have an apartment available, would you like to see it?" says the officer-in-charge.

We are taken to see this so-called apartment right next to the hospital. It is a converted nurses' barracks, vintage WW II. The H-shaped building sprawls across a grassy field and accommodates six families. Passing through a large screened porch, we walk into a spacious open room and look down a seemingly endless hall. On either side are *six* bedrooms, a dining room, kitchen and the strangest bathroom you'll ever see in a home. It has two sinks with mirrors, two toilets in stalls, a shower, a bathtub and room for a washer and dryer.

Though it isn't *exactly* what we imagined when we pictured our first real house, it seems to be the perfect place. There will be plenty of room for our three children, the Navy pays for and maintains it, and we will certainly enjoy the company of other families living in the same complex.

On August 12, 1969 several weeks after I sat watching the first man walk on the Moon, our third child, Amy, is born. Harry Jr. and Lori rejoin the family in our new "house," and we settle into what is for us a bountiful period. For the first time in our marriage, we have the luxury of both a decent salary and a schedule which allows Harry time with the family.

My time is filled with children, officers' wives' duties and enjoying the benefits of life on a Naval Base. I also enjoy an occasional "read" when I can spare a moment. A physician friend of ours offers me a book called *Day of the Dolphin* by Robert Merle.

"You like to read about weird stuff," he jokes. "I think you would enjoy this."

The book is a fictional account of a research project in which dolphins are taught to speak. The story is an exciting and absorbing one, but it is the dolphins themselves who completely captivate me in a way I can't describe. I read a page or two, then get so excited about what I'm reading that I get up from my chair and pace around the room! I read further, can't sit still, get up and pace again. This is strange, very strange!

Where I am, we call this an Epiphany, a funny word meaning that a light is suddenly turned on in a person's life and they see things in a new way; they wake up and pay attention. Oh, you have that word too? Don't you just love it?

Libby Layne has become very excited about the dolphins, but doesn't yet know she is being introduced to a most important piece of her life's puzzle.

For reasons I don't understand, my fascination with the dolphins sends me to libraries, searching for information about their lives, history — anything and everything related to them.

Dolphins, I learn, have lived on earth in their present form for 40,000,000 years. From the earliest time in history, stories have been told of the special bond between dolphins and humans. In Greek and Roman times, dolphins were thought to be emissaries of various gods in whom the people believed. Ancient drawings in caves, paintings on pottery, and legends passed down orally from generation to generation tell of their unique place in the animal world. Many are the tales of dolphins saving human lives in the ocean.

I am amazed when I read dolphins have a brain larger than that of a human and are extremely intelligent. They do communicate, though they are physically incapable of speaking as they had in the novel I read. They are able to learn sign language and both comprehend and react to changes in word order or syntax. Until recently this was a skill thought to be unique to humans. When a dolphin looks into a mirror, he gestures and makes faces as he watches himself. He appears to know he is looking at himself, not at another dolphin. This would mean he has self-awareness, another trait common to animals of high intelligence. Everything I was learning about these incredible mammals left me wanting to know more.

For the next two years, Libby Layne gathers information about dolphins from books, magazines and TV. She reads one day of a woman in Florida who works with special children swimming with dolphins. This doesn't make a big impression then, but I know this is an important connection to events in what you call "the future." I enjoy knowing special secrets like this, though sometimes it's very hard not to give them away too soon. It is important, you see, that I only guide her to make her own discoveries.

July, 1972

After two enjoyable years in the Navy, our family returns home to Virginia. With the two older children in school, and no need or desire for an outside-the-home career, I have time to do volunteer work. I become involved at the children's school, with their swim team, their carpools, and other activities throughout the community. While we were in the Navy, I had no opportunity to use my musical talents. In fact, I haven't sung a note in two years! Happily, I begin singing again in a church choir and the community chorus. I am asked to do solo work as well as to perform in musical theater. At the local fine arts center I organize a children's chorus which I direct. This frenzy of activity fills the time I have alone, as Harry's new medical practice builds and he is rarely home. We all miss our time together, after being spoiled by his freedom of the Navy years.

My time alone also rekindles my need for spiritual nurturing. We had joined a little Episcopal church in Millington and had gone to church as a family, but my interest in any spiritual growth has taken a Naval holiday along with my music.

Back in a community setting, in addition to my involvement in church, I join several Bible study groups. Though I want a structured religious study, I soon feel smothered by those who have many of the same attitudes about truth to which I was exposed as a child in the Church of the Brethren. The truth they believe is inflexible and infallible. There is no room for the possibility of other truths outside their narrow views. I had been born into the Christian faith, and as an adult had chosen to live from that perspective. Yet, I have also allowed myself the freedom to read about other religions and philosophies, finding in each of them certain truths which have enhanced my Christian beliefs. Lately I have been seeking an understanding of what that means with respect to my life's purpose.

I am always excited when I see Libby Layne begin to search for answers. It is at these times I can be the most help to her. When she starts seeking, we here make certain she finds.

Her musical activities in the community have given Libby Layne quite a bit of recognition. When people say how much they enjoy and appreciate what she does it makes her feel special. For most of her life she has used her musical gifts for her own enjoyment and to entertain. Certainly, there is nothing wrong with doing this, but these same gifts are also meant to be used in service to others. This was one of the lessons I taught my parents during my mission on earth.

A seed was planted in Libby Layne's soul when she heard that part of my story.

It is a joyful thing to know that even though she never met me when I was on earth, still my mission reached her.

The seed planted so long ago, was ready to sprout. All it needed was a little sun. The sun came in the form of a television movie. The movie was called Son Rise.*"*

*"A coincidence is merely a situation
in which God chooses to remain anonymous."*
(anonymous)

Spring, 1981

While watching television one evening, I happen to see a movie called *Son Rise*. The movie tells the true story of a little boy who has autism. Through a process of love and acceptance, his parents help him return from his world of autism to the world of his family.

I have never heard the word autism and know nothing about how it affects people.

Something about the little boy and the way his parents are with him touches me, and my heart and eyes fill to overflowing. I watch spellbound as the parents, seated in front of the little boy, imitate his every move. Speaking in hushed, loving voices, they rock their bodies back and forth, back and forth as he does. They give him a ball which he spins round and round on the floor with his hand, eyes focused intently on his task. The parents then mirror his ball-twirling, quietly encouraging him to look at *them,* to enter *their* world, yet accepting him exactly where he is at that moment.

I can't explain the strong emotions I feel and the incredible empathy I have with the family on the screen. Again, as with the dolphins, I feel compelled to look for more information about autism.

Searching the library, I learn that little is known about this strange disorder. In the 1940's Dr. Leo Kanner observed that certain children shared the same odd behaviors: difficulty relating to, communicating with, and not wanting to be around people, difficulty relating to objects in a "normal" way, repetitive and ritualistic behaviors, an aversion to being held or touched, having the need to have everything exactly the same all the time, and being very sensitive to loud sounds. To this group of behaviors (syndrome) he gave the name "autism." The cause is unknown and there is no cure — only treatment, and precious little of that. It is seen four times more often in boys than girls, but affects all races of people throughout the world.

In the early years of the study of autism, one doctor stated that it was caused by cold and unloving mothers or, as they were unkindly called, "refrigerator moms." Though this proved to be completely untrue, for years many parents blamed themselves for their children's behaviors. Physicians advised parents to send their autistic children to institutions. So little was known about this disorder that treatment was often cruel. Behavior modification techniques were used in many cases, assuming that these children could chose to change their behavior at will. Children were sometimes restrained with ropes, had food withheld, were left in corners where they beat their heads against walls. They were grossly misunderstood and left to live out their lives with no hope, no dignity.

For almost forty years, the medical world continued to be baffled by autism. Families were given no hope that their autistic child would ever improve or recover. It was generally accepted that autism was an emotional or psychological disorder rather than a physical one.

As more was learned about mental illness and mental retardation, parents began taking an active role in learning about autism. Along with many parents of children with other disabilities, they chose to keep their autistic children at home, observing in many cases that a home atmosphere had a positive effect on their behavior. As a result, parents of these children began sharing information with each other, eventually becoming advocates who demanded that doctors and the public take a new look at autism and alternative therapies. Such was the couple in the film *Son Rise*.

Even today, the majority of medical doctors offer little encouragement or hope for individuals with autism. Having seen *Son Rise*, I feel there *is* hope; I believe there are options. Something inside me is saying, "I can do what those parents did; I *want* to do what they did." This desire to be involved with these children is very intense, very passionate. Yet I have no idea from where it comes; it is a mystery to me.

I continue my exploration of the causes of and treatments for autism. I read every piece of written material that crosses my path on the subject. Each time I hear the word autism on the radio or TV, I listen attentively, forming my own theories concerning the disorder. It reminds me of my obsession with dolphins years before.

In a television program reviewing innovative treatments for the mentally retarded, I hear a name that sounds familiar, yet I can't place it. A woman in Florida named Dr. Betsy Smith has observed that children with Down's Syndrome and other forms of mental retardation seem to benefit when they swim with dolphins. In her own research study she has observed the same positive results when *autistic* children swim with *dolphins*. The appearance of two of my abiding passions in the same context causes a reaction that is no less than explosive! Unable to sit still, I jump up and begin pacing around the room. I am onto something important!

You might say that two of Libby Layne's Epiphanies just Epiphanized! (I just made up that word myself.)

At this moment she has only begun to make connections. She has not realized that the dolphins and autistic children will be her teachers in solving the mystery of the Sound of the Dolphin's Psalm. In truth, she doesn't yet know there is a mystery. But her inborn "spirit of tenacity" does and so do I. I will continue to guide her to other teachers, to other puzzle pieces which will one day fit together.

With a little help from me, Libby Layne has realized it is time to use her musical gift in a new way. After her discovery of the world of autism, she wonders if there might be a way of using her music with people in that world. She remembers a friend who is a music therapist. She knows that music is used by these therapists as a tool for helping people with all sorts of problems — mental retardation, mental illness, alcoholism, the elderly and many more. Perhaps children with autism could benefit too? Certain autistic people have amazing musical talent and others simply enjoy music. Could this be a way she might use her music differently?

Her friend works at The Lynchburg Training Center, one of those institutions where people like me were sent to live before much was known about Down's Syndrome. There were others sent there, people with problems doctors knew little about: brain-damage, schizophrenia, Cerebral Palsy, birth defects and various mental problems. Early on, it was called "The Colony," as if it were a place for lepers or something. Back then, most people were afraid of anyone with mental retardation and didn't want to be around them. It wasn't that doctors and parents were cruel, they just didn't know any better. Many people who could have stayed at home and been loved just like I was, spent their lives in that place. Through the years, professionals learned more about mental retardation and mental illness. Now the Training Center only admits residents who need special care they can receive nowhere else. Humans are getting better at understanding.

I wonder sometimes why time on earth is measured in a long line. While waiting for the truth to catch up with people who need to know it, others get hurt. Here, we see everything, all at once. I don't know why it's different on earth, but I'm sure that there is a good reason. There always is.

Her music therapist friend, Hadley, is pleased when Libby Layne calls, asking to help him with his program at the Training Center. He invites her to come to observe his music classes with the residents. A time is set.

IV
Duet

September, 1981

I like September. It is a beginning-kind-of-month for me. For so many years school began then for me, first as a student, then as a teacher, the wife of a student and finally the mother of students. There are feelings of anticipation after three months of vacation, new school supplies being gathered, new schedules being planned, new goals being set. It's always a time when I like to begin new projects and make fresh starts. This September is no exception.

I drive to my first session with Hadley at the Training Center. I was completely confident that this was what I wanted to do — until this moment. Now I find that I am uneasy at the prospect of being with so many who are profoundly retarded. I have only been exposed to them at the Fine Arts Center when they were brought to concerts. Their weird, mournful sounds and bizarre behaviors always made me feel uncomfortable.

Again I wonder why I have such a passionate desire to do this, to help these individuals. It is quite common for family members or friends of those who have mental retardation to become involved, to become advocates for this population. However, this does not apply at all in my case, having rarely been exposed to anyone with these problems. I utter a little prayer for extra understanding and compassion as I enter Building #30 where Hadley is waiting.

I enter a large room called the "day hall" where people of all ages sit in wheelchairs, lie on mattresses, or wander about. I have a feeling of having landed on another planet in the midst of alien beings. The bodies resemble the human form, but have mutated limbs, gross distortions. Heads too large for bodies are propped on pillows or headrests; limbs too small hang limply, unusable. I hear a rasping breath behind me. Turning, I gasp as I come face to face with a small creature of a boy with only half a face, who breathes through a reddened and oozing trachea tube in his neck. A familiar, sour smell permeates the air; what *is* that? I then recognize it as the odor of soiled baby diapers. Though most of these aliens are adults, many are unable to use the toilet and are diapered. There are eerie noises, grunts, cries, laughter, and screams. Aides help the aliens with medication, eating, and other activities they are incapable of doing for themselves. One of the aliens reaches out for Hadley, who gently takes her hand and greets her with kind words. He weaves his way through the day hall, talking with and touching each resident in a quiet, loving way.

Using him as a model, I begin greeting the aliens. Ill at ease and cautious, I meet one after another of these strange beings, finding, after a time, that my perception of them as aliens changes. They aren't aliens at all. Though their appearance, their outer shells may be grotesque, it takes only a smile, the touch of a hand, a kind word, to transform them. They only wish to be treated like humans. They only need to be loved.

Hadley begins his music class. Mesmerized, I watch as he handles each resident with loving care. He patiently encourages one to beat a drum, another to hit a bell or clap his hands to the music he plays. These skills, so simple and easy to the average person, are extraordinary and wonderful to these people. The music brings smiles and laughter to those trapped in bodies that can't manage the simplest tasks. The music brightens their dreary world.

After class, Hadley leads me down a hall to the music room. On the way I hear a pitiful wailing accompanied by the ring of jingle bells. Sitting in a wheelchair back in a corner, is a young boy.

"This is Pringle," Hadley says.

Pringle doesn't look up, doesn't seem to know that anyone is there. Ringing the set of jingle bells in his ear with his hand, he nods his head back and forth in a rhythmic pattern. The neck of his T-shirt is chewed and wet; he is lost in a world of his own. He is quite beautiful, with dark silky hair and dark brown eyes that stare off into the distance. I immediately am reminded of the little boy in *Son Rise*.

"Is he autistic?"

"No," Hadley says, "he was brain-damaged in a fall when he was a baby."

I don't question this but am intrigued by the similarities I see in Pringle's behaviors and what I know of autism. A voice inside tells me this one is special; *he* is the reason I am here.

Hadley arranges permission for me to assist him and the other music therapist with his program. I begin coming once a week, working with various residents, including Pringle. I enjoy everyone but soon find myself spending more time with him. His favorable response to me and my music is drawing me into his world. If only I can draw him out into mine.

Each time I arrive, Pringle is doing exactly the same thing he did the first time I met him. Sitting in his wheelchair, he cries, ringing the jingle bells in his ear as he nods his head back and forth; the aides say sometimes he has been doing this for hours.

Even though Pringle isn't diagnosed autistic, I begin treating him as if he were. The autistic boy in *Son Rise*, his parents believed, went into a world of his own, escaping, for some reason, the real world. To become a part of "his world" they joined him in his repetitive behaviors or "isms" as they called them, accepting and loving him just as he was. This is the attitude I adopt as I begin using music with Pringle.

My first task when I arrive is to calm Pringle and quiet his crying. I discover that playing *Twinkle, Twinkle Little Star* like a music box on the top keys of the piano gets his attention. The minute he stops crying, I take away the jingle bells. He listens for a little while, then goes back to his world, rocking his head. He likes to listen to music on a tape recorder, but this doesn't keep his attention as well as the piano or when I sing. I notice that even though he doesn't look directly at me or at anything else, he looks away when I try to make eye contact. Many children with autism refuse to make eye contact with other people, even their parents. I had been told Pringle was blind. If Pringle were blind as they say, why would he look away?

45

Because I am a volunteer, I hesitate to pry into areas that are none of my business, but I do become curious about Pringle's history. As I gradually gain the trust of the staff, they begin sharing information about him.

He has been at the Training Center since he was six years old; he is now eleven. When he was several months old, he had a brain hemorrhage, cause unknown. Pringle has a twin brother with none of Pringle's problems and an older brother and sister. During the first years after his brain damage, he was kept at home with the family. When it became too difficult with three other young children, he went to live with a loving Mennonite family. When they moved away and could no longer keep him, the decision was made to send him to the Training Center. What a painful decision this must have been for his parents. They visit him regularly and take great interest in his very limited progress. He can't walk or talk. The muscles of his arms and legs are contracted with spasms which cause him pain. He cries or screams most of the time and seems to have no interest at all in the outside world or any desire to learn more about it. He does seem to recognize his family when they come. The staff at the Training Center say they are very nice people and hope I will have the opportunity to meet them when they visit.

Several weeks after coming regularly to see Pringle, I start a session by playing the piano and singing. Pringle stops what he is doing and reaches out for the piano, as if he wants to play. This is the first time he has shown interest in anything outside his world other than his jingle bells.

This is only the beginning! The next week, he bangs on the keys with both hands, smiling, as I play and sing. I try teaching him to beat the drum. At first all he wants to do is chew on the stick. It isn't long before he is beating the drum, shaking his head in time with the music, and smiling all over his face. I sing a variety of songs including *Oom-Pa-Pa* from *Oliver, I Love You a Bushel and a Peck, Twinkle, Twinkle* and *Jesus Loves Me*.

He is very particular about what he likes and dislikes. He likes hearing the top keys on the piano but not the low ones. He likes *I Love You a Bushel and a Peck, Twinkle, Twinkle, Oom-Pa-Pa,* and *Jesus Loves Me.* He does not like *Doe a Deer.*

Certain noises seem to bother him more than others, causing him to retreat into his world to shut them out. There are certainly abundant noises in the day hall which might bother him if he is sensitive to sound.

I also experiment with musical games of all kinds with Pringle. I teach him to pat-a-cake, and soon, when I enter the day hall and greet him with, "Hello Pringle," he begins clapping as a signal for me to sing. When I do, he laughs and claps even more. One day I ask Pringle, "Do you want to play the piano?" He immediately reaches out for the piano.

How in the world can he understand what I just said if he is profoundly retarded or a 'Big 0' as one evaluator had put it?

I always speak to Pringle as if he understands every word I say. He seems to respond positively to this, and though he may not understand the words, I am positive he comprehends my intention to communicate intimately with him. The music, together with the love and attention I give him, brings him further and further out of his shell into the outer world. He is improving in other areas of his life also, even when I'm not around. He now goes to Hadley's music class, where he participates by clapping and nodding his head to music that is played. His incessant wailing has decreased, and because he is more alert, the aides take more of an interest in him. No longer do they allow him to cry for long periods in a corner, because they know he is capable of responding to their attention.

The bond between Pringle and me grows stronger as he responds to my music, attention and love. I now go to the Center at least twice a week. For a month I intensify my visits, going five or six days in a row. The staff teases me about the amount of time I spend with him, that I am spoiling him, but are pleased at his progress. They "report" to me any new behaviors which might help in my work with him.

Although I am aware Pringle isn't diagnosed autistic, he does, in many ways, *act* autistic. What relationship does this have to his brain damage? I discuss this with Hadley and give him the book *Son Rise* to read over the weekend.

On Monday, after reading the book, Hadley greets me with a huge smile, a thumbs-up and a "Right on!" He is excited about looking at Pringle's behaviors in this new and different way.

He takes the information to Pringle's "Staffing" — a meeting held to discuss a resident's progress among the people who work with him. Being both a layman and a volunteer, I am surprised and delighted that my suggestions are being taken seriously.

Today, I wheel Pringle into the music room and neither play the piano nor make a sound. The minute he gets near the piano, he reaches out and begins playing it. "Playing it" might be a slight exaggeration in terms, but to me it is a celestial concerto!

I suspect that Pringle may not be as blind as the staff team thinks. I am told he is "tactiley" blind, meaning his eyes may see something, but his brain does not compute what it is. How, then, I wonder, does he know, without any sounds, that there is a piano in the room *and* how to play it?

Excitedly, I report the news of Pringle's "recital" to Hadley. From Hadley, the story goes to Pringle's staff team which decides his eyesight will be retested. The results of the test are positive. Pringle *can* see, at least a little! He is put in a special program for the blind or partially blind who can be helped. By this time, I am considered an unofficial member of his "team," sharing information with everyone involved with Pringle.

During the next four years, I become an integral part of Pringle's world. I meet his parents, who give me permission to take Pringle out of the building, off the property and, after a time, home with me for the day and sometimes to spend the night. These times together are filled with new discoveries for him, stimulating his every sense: he sees the world whiz by from the window of my car as we ride to my house, he feels the soft fur of my cats, the wiry hair of my dog, he tastes a McDonald's cheeseburger and french fries, he smells a log fire in the fireplace and spends the night in a room where he hears only a peaceful silence.

His parents are pleased when they see his progress. They are relieved that he appears to be happier in his living environment and that he has someone near who loves him and is giving him extra attention.

He experiments making different sounds with his voice, as if trying to communicate. In all areas of his life at the Center, he relates more to the world outside his own. Some days are better than others, but Pringle's good days encourage me to try new techniques with him. In everything I do with him I always use the approach I had seen in the movie *Son Rise*, that of unconditional love and acceptance.

I dream of Pringle often. In the dreams there is healing and wholeness. One in particular stays with me. In the dream, we are at the Training School. We are outside, and as I push him in his wheelchair among the trees he begins looking right at me. His gaze is intense, and he makes eye contact for a long time. He begins smiling, then laughing, then talking and singing. He doesn't sing the songs I have sung to him; he is singing new songs. In the dream Pringle appears older and wiser than I. He is the adult, I am the child. He also appears to be teasing me, as if he knows a great secret. I sense that somehow he has been fooling everyone, including me, all along. He *walks* inside to the day hall where he *talks* with the staff. Everyone is amazed, and I am ecstatic. As the dream ends I keep saying, "It is God who has done this." It is important to me that they understand I was only an instrument. God is responsible for this wonderful miracle!

Our relationship grows as he improves, and I find myself praying he will someday be well enough to go home. I believe this is possible, and I refuse to give up this hope. It almost feels like my mission.

I am sorry she will be disappointed, but hope and pray as she might, this was not to be. Pringle is only a part of what she calls her "mission," while my own mission is to guide her to her next puzzle piece.

As the years go by, Pringle retreats again to his own isolated world. Not only has he stopped making progress, he is going back to where he had been four years earlier. When Libby Layne visits him, he is less and less interested in her and her world.

He is moved into a building where there is no music room or piano. The day hall is noisy, and there is little privacy for Libby Layne and Pringle to be alone. He is a teenager now and has become too heavy for her to carry around as she had before. This means she can't take him home for visits. Libby Layne becomes discouraged. She doesn't want to desert him, but wonders if everything that can be done has been done. Her visits become infrequent, which makes her feel guilty. She worries that she may have done too little or given up too soon. Had her mission failed?

But I knew Pringle was the one with the mission. He had come to teach Libby Layne certain lessons. And what had been his mission? What lessons had he taught her in those four years?

Even I don't know everything he taught. Each angel knows why he or she comes to earth, but can't be positive of another's mission. I do know some of the lessons.

He taught her that a deformity, a disability is only the outer shell; beneath it there is always somebody "home." He drew on her gift of tenacity, insisting that she never give up seeking the person he was inside his own shell. He taught her to believe in the truth she saw with her heart and to stand up for that truth. The lesson she most needed to learn for her special journey was this: music alone is a powerful healing tool, but its power is without limits when enhanced by love and acceptance.

Near the end of her regular visits, she commented that Pringle seemed to have no concept of time except the present. When she came, he acknowledged her presence and smiled when she sang, but there was not the sense of a continuing relationship that she had felt with him before. He no longer cried when she left, and whether it had been a week, a month or a year between visits, there was no indication that he missed her. Though this saddened her, it did make it easier for her to move on. I knew Pringle was letting her go; it was time.

It is September again...

V
Interlude

September, 1984

This September I became *Elizabeth.*

It is again that time of year when something gets stirred up in my being and I launch into new territory. The change, or in my case the reinstatement, of my given name has something to do with where I am in my personal development.

There is a culture of aboriginal people in Australia who rename themselves periodically throughout their lifetime. Sometimes this name refers to one's new duties or skills, or it may reflect a maturation process and how one feels about oneself. For some reason, I feel more like an Elizabeth now. When meeting a new person, I introduce myself as Elizabeth, though to everyone else I am still Libby or Libby Layne. Perhaps I believe I will be taken more seriously with a more dignified name, or maybe I just like the sound of it. It does have a certain resonance.

My work with Pringle at the Training Center has come to an end with some disappointment and sadness. The miracle for which I had hoped was apparently not to be, or at least not as I had envisioned it. Occasionally I visit him at the Training Center, but he seems lost to me. He is more content and has ceased his endless crying, but he has returned to his own world. I only hope it is a peaceful one.

Amy is preparing to graduate from high school, and both Harry Jr. and Lori are in college. Harry Sr. is still immersed in his medical practice. In the past year, without knowing why, I have been steadily decreasing my volunteer work in the community. I sense that I am opening space for something else, something important, though I have yet to discover what it is.

"What are you doing today?" I ask Patricia, my longtime friend and neighbor.

"I'm going to register for my counseling degree at Lynchburg College."

Without so much as an "Oh, really," I state emphatically, "I am too."

With that, I march myself out to the College, register for classes, apply for a student loan and return as a full-time student to earn a Masters Degree in Counseling.

Perhaps my "Elizabeth Self" is responsible for the absolute certainty that *this* is the "something important" for which I have cleared the space. The decision is not as impulsive as it might appear.

During the years I worked with Pringle, I observed the difficulties faced by his family. Parents of children with disabilities have few resources available to help them cope with a myriad of complex problems and mixed emotions. In accepting the reality of a special child, parents must grieve the loss of certain hopes and dreams, much the same as if grieving the death of a child. As a counselor for these parents, I would be in a position to encourage fresh hopes, to guide them in developing new dreams.

Not since 1962, when I graduated from the University of Richmond, have I been associated with the academic world. My degree in Music Education and voice had come easily. I am somewhat anxious about a curriculum which has no connection whatsoever to my natural talent and wonder if I am in over my head. I soon find that going back to school at the age of forty-four has a completely different focus than the college of my youth. The absence of countless extracurricular activities and the *vital* social obligation of dating, opens to me a whole new perspective of higher education. I have been learning on my own for years, and as I enter this formal educational setting, I find it stimulating and challenging. I am a capable graduate student and gain new confidence in my intellect and my abilities.

A graduation requirement of the Masters of Education Degree in counseling is participation in a practicum. Since I am preparing to become a counselor for parents of special children, I devise my own practicum to meet my particular interests. I learn of a national organization called Parent to Parent. This group has met with great success in encouraging parents of special children to help each other by sharing experiences. It will be my task to develop a Parent to Parent group locally. I am required to have an organization and an advisor under which to work. The ARC (Association for Retarded Citizens) of Central Virginia, part of a nationwide organization addressing the needs of those with all forms of disability, agrees to this. They are delighted with the concept of a support system for the parents they serve. In setting up this program, I meet many parents of special children and make contacts in the medical and educational circles in the community. As I complete my practicum and take my comprehensives, I feel confident that I am prepared for the field which I have chosen.

My graduation ceremony, complete with cap and gown, is attended by all my children, my husband and my mother-in-law, all of whom are quite proud of me. Afterwards Harry asks, "Now that you have this degree, what are you going to do with it?"

"I don't know yet, but I'll know when it comes along."

Spring, 1986

"I have the perfect thing for you! I think you'll want to be involved. When can you meet with me about it?" says the voice excitedly over the phone.

A new school for students with learning difficulties is being organized by a friend, and I am asked to be part of it. Initially, my interest is minimal; this isn't exactly what I have in mind, but it does have possibilities. At the school I would have an opportunity to use my new counseling skills and to teach music. I am also asked to become involved financially and be a member of the founding Board of Directors. I am not at all sure about this. It is a huge commitment of both time and money, not to mention that, for the first time in many years, I am being asked to go to a "real" job. Is this what I really want? What about the autistic children, what about the dolphins? Am I really following my heart or going off on a tangent to please someone else? This will require a prayerful decision.

While earning our masters degrees, my friend Patricia and I often fantasized about our future together as counselors. As graduation neared, another longtime friend and fellow student joined our discussions. Now, as I make my decision about the new school, I have a sincere desire to work with these two friends. Like me, neither of them has considered a school setting, but each has skills, in addition to counseling, which would benefit the school. I present the idea of their participation to the woman who originally approached me, then discuss it with my two counselor friends.

At first, they too hesitate to commit to something so different from what we had envisioned. The three of us meet with the two women who created the idea of the school; one has an educational background, the other an expertise in mental health and administration. As we look at the counseling services that could be offered at the school, our excitement mounts. If counseling were to be of equal importance to academics in this psycho-educational model, there could be individual, group and family counseling. Like no other school in our area, we could meet the complex needs of both the student with learning difficulties and his family. The idea grows and develops and the decision is made. The five of us will establish a school to be opened in the fall.

Everyone is confident this will, indeed, be a special school. In addition to academics and counselling, there will be a strong emphasis on art, music, and drama. Above all, there will be an abiding atmosphere of unconditional love and acceptance. This multifaceted approach will enable a student to have a more positive school experience, enhance his self-esteem and nurture his soul. The teacher-student ratio will be small, and each student will be treated with dignity as a unique individual. We hope to serve a wide range of educational and emotional needs. I am assured that, in the future, there will be a place for autistic children.

After prayerful consideration, I commit to the project. I still have a few reservations, but chalk them up to nervousness about moving into completely new territory. This might be the culmination of all that has gone before.

The planning begins in the spring, and, amazingly, by September we open with twelve students, varying in age from six to sixteen, each with special problems and special gifts.

The fears of my freedom being constricted dissipate as I excitedly create an innovative program. I use music in my counseling sessions and counseling in my music classes. I discover that music enhances both communicating feelings and teaching facts. I assist teachers, using music as a learning tool in academic subjects such as history, geography, biology and ecology.

In music class, older students are exposed to Mozart by studying his life as a "funky genius," then come to my house to watch the movie *Amadeus* and eat popcorn. I come to know them individually and they see me not only as teacher/counselor, but as a person in my home setting. It forges close relationships and an atmosphere of trust.

Younger students go on a scavenger hike to listen to sounds in the outside world: birds, cars, train whistles, fire engine sirens. "I didn't know there was so much sound," they exclaim. They learn to listen, to pay attention, to be observant. There is a prize for the student who lists the most sounds. During Halloween I introduce them to the scary story of *The Phantom of the Opera,* and then, before they know it, they are listening to an opera and *loving* it.

As a special project, the older students, the drama teacher and I decide to produce an adaptation of the musical play *You're a Good Man Charlie Brown.* Students who have difficulty even *reading,* memorize lines, lyrics, and stage directions. They work together as a team, helping each other master their parts, putting together costumes and gathering props. Finally, they astound their parents, teachers and friends with a performance that gives them a sense of accomplishment and pride in themselves. The arts are a vital part of their education here and a means of boosting their self-esteem.

We all learn about sound vibration and how music is made. We experiment with how music can change their moods and feelings, helping them to relax.

Exposing them to a variety of music styles, I strike a bargain with the teenagers: if they listen to *my* music, I will listen to *theirs.* They are given an opportunity to explain the importance of the music they like, and I broaden their musical experience by explaining my own tastes. They draw pictures to music, move to music, play and sing music. It is a time for learning and discovery for both the students and their teacher.

One of my most fascinating musical discoveries comes from a sea mammal. It is not the dolphins this time but the songs of the Humpback Whale which have been recorded in the open ocean by a scientist with an underwater microphone. They can be correctly called "songs," since the whales repeat the same sequence of notes over and over again, adding to their personal melody each year. Combining these songs with instruments, Paul Winter has created a magical world of sound. This music is incredibly beautiful, haunting and very different from anything the students or I have ever heard.

The whalesong has a calming effect on students and staff alike. I was discovering that not only music, but the sounds of nature are powerful healing tools. Some staff members, experiencing positive feelings, mention that the sounds put them into a meditative state.

The students become fascinated with the whalesong and want to know more about the animals who sing them. Together we explore the world of whales, and I am once again immersed in a treasure hunt for information. I encourage them to do as I do: read, watch, listen and learn as much as they are able. They learn that dolphins are actually small whales, giving me a perfect opportunity to share my knowledge and excitement concerning them. The school is providing a setting for combining my three abiding interests — music, special children and dolphins. I feel completely satisfied that the decision to be involved in the school was a good one. It is something I am *meant* to do.

Out of this sense of "call" associated with the school's formation, comes my personal belief that the school belongs to God; we are only the caretakers. The other two counselors have the same belief. Though there is no religious affiliation or teaching of any kind at the school, we feel that we are overseers of sacred space. Each weekend before the students come in on Monday morning, the three of us meet at the school. We then go to each of the rooms, asking a blessing and praying for love and light to abide there during the next week for everyone.

The first year is a peaceful, wonderful year. Everyone who comes in the door says, "I can feel the love here." There is much joy, fun and laughter ringing through the halls of this truly special school. There dwells here an atmosphere of acceptance, security and what feels like a touch of the holy.

During the second year something happens, changing this feeling. Teachers become unhappy, and there are disagreements among members of the Board. There are money problems and personnel problems. Joy and laughter ring less and less through the halls, and the fun is fading. The original dream for the school is being replaced by something different — nothing negative really, just different.

For so many years, I experienced the freedom of being a volunteer, the luxury of not *having* to work. Now, I find myself with teaching and counseling duties, and as President of the Board, administrative responsibilities as well. I am in the middle of much of the turmoil, mediating disagreements. Not only is this more involvement and pressure than I expected, there is a new sense of having strayed from the path on which I was set by the forces guiding me thus far. Perhaps the school is providing lessons for my journey, not its culmination.

In the fall of my third year at the school, I reduce my involvement significantly. I remain as President of the Board but am at the school only Monday through Wednesday. I continue counseling students with whom I worked in previous years, taking on no additional ones. My music classes are still the most satisfying aspect of my work, and I become more and more interested in the powerful effects of music. I observe that not only music, but certain sounds help students with special needs. I had also seen this in my years with Pringle at the Training Center. Following my usual pattern, I head to the library, seeking to expand my knowledge of music and sound therapies. Finding little information there, I decide to take a college course.

I learn that Radford University is the only school in the state which offers a graduate course in music therapy. I enroll in a class which meets once a week in the evening. Each Wednesday after teaching at the school, I drive to Radford, attend class, spend the night with a friend there, then return the next morning.

The class has only seven graduate students, all of whom have undergraduate degrees in music therapy. The music therapist who teaches the course is quite knowledgeable in the subject of sound vibrations as a healing tool and an aid to spiritual growth. He is also interested in Transpersonal Psychology, a more spiritual view of psychology. I am fascinated, and, as with dolphins and autism, I completely absorb myself in readings on the subject.

I learn that from the beginning of time, in all cultures, music and sound have been used routinely as tools for healing of physical, psychological and spiritual ills. These methods of using sound vibration, forgotten through the years, are now being studied and used again. I am reminded of the whalesong I play at the school. The power of these songs affects us all profoundly. Could there be a connection to the autistic children or the dolphins?

Though it may seem to Libby Layne that she has "strayed from her path," I know that she is right on course. Her love of and talent for music has been active, her compassion for children with disabilities is still just as strong, and her "spirit of tenacity" will continue to lead her forward to new connections between the dolphins and sound therapy. The path sometimes just takes a detour or two.

Heal The World With Sound

The Universe, is Vibration
It began with Sound, God's Incantation
Air Blowing
Fire Glowing
Water Flowing
Earth Knowing
Heal the World with Sound!

The Earth, filled with Vibration
Cries out to all who'll hear, "Rejuvenation!"
Sky Smogging
Tree Logging
Sea Dying
Child Crying
Heal the World with Sound!

Humankind, joined by Vibration
The Beat of Human Hearts from every Nation
Freedom Calling
Wall Falling
Peace Brinking
Arm Linking
Heal the World with Sound!

The Body moves to Vibration
With Dancing Feet, in Celebration
Band Playing
Hip Swaying
Hand Clapping
Soul Rapping
Heal the World with Sound!

The Soul is Pure Vibration
ReSounding to God's Incantation
A Psalm of Love for all things Living
A Psalm of Thanks and of Forgiving
A Psalm we Sing Together in Harmony
Heal the World with Sound!

VI
Recitative and Aria

Once upon my daily walk,
On a spot I'd passed a thousand times,
A man sits, head in hands.
I do not pass to the other side,
But stop and ask, "Is all well?"
His answer to my concern,
The violence all women fear.
Time stops, my world stops, life stops
In that moment.
But in that moment there was another
Than the two of us.
Renewing time, renewing my world, renewing my life.
And today, as again I passed that spot
Upon my daily walk,
Daises grow.
And I Praise God for Grace and for Daisies.

September, 1988

"What a day! There's not a cloud in the sky," would be my dad's comment on this particular morning. The bright autumn sun is shining, its warmth only slightly diminished by a trace of brisk, fall air. There couldn't be a more ideal Saturday for my three-mile jaunt up to Boonsboro Road and back.

At about 9:00 AM I don my blue striped walking shorts, JMU sweat-shirt and my cross-trainer shoes. Then, in my anticipatory September-state-of mind, I stride energetically out the driveway. Harry, "playing" with his yard work, waves good-bye.

I have walked this familiar route for ten years: John Scott to Old Trents Ferry, Old Trents Ferry to Trents Ferry, Trents Ferry to its end. At the Stop sign on Boonsboro Road, I stretch out tightened muscles, then return home the same way. It takes me about forty-five minutes.

Today when I reach the end of Trents Ferry, nearing the Stop sign, I notice a young man seated on a landscape timber next to the sidewalk, head in his hands. Tapping him on the shoulder to get his attention, I ask if he is all right. Speaking to a stranger, especially one who may need help, is not unusual for me. On this stretch of road, I frequently converse with workmen who are courteous and friendly.

"I'm fine," he says, "I'm just waiting for my work partner to come."

I continue to the end of the street, do my routine stretches at the Stop sign, turn around and begin walking toward home. The man has been out of sight, but as I walk back, I see him still seated at the same spot. I pass him saying, "It's a beautiful day, isn't it?"

Suddenly, the man stands up, grabs my arm and roughly twists it behind my back. There is something pointed sticking in my back, but I haven't yet determined what it is. He begins walking me up the street, holding my arm tightly behind me.

"Don't scream, I have a gun." I have discerned by now that it is not a gun, only his finger and tell him as much.

"Let's go to your house."

"I don't live near here."

"I know where you live, I've been watching you."

My mind is racing, scarcely keeping pace with the beating of my heart. Thoughts, like single frames of a home movie, blink on the screen of my brain: "I am on a busy street... this is a safe town... it is broad daylight... this is Saturday morning... there are always people walking, biking and running along here... someone will see I'm in trouble... where in heaven's name are the people?"

I don't scream or struggle, positive a car will drive by, a walker or runner will pass me. I never come this way without meeting at least one person who knows me. But there is nothing, no one! It's as though the world has suddenly and completely emptied, leaving in it only this stranger and me.

I remain uncannily composed. My thinking is sharp and quick. I am acutely aware that I am in a dangerous situation. Unless someone appears quickly, I will need some plan for escape. I have read that one way of dealing with an attacker is to remain calm and attempt to dissuade him from his intention. I have always been especially good at talking and decide to try this approach.

Interrupting my train of thought he asks, "Do you have any money?"

"No, I never carry any money when I walk. Why don't you take my watch and ring?"

I am hoping robbery is his only motive. I frantically scan the road and sidewalk, waiting for someone, anyone to rescue me. Not one car! Not one person!

Libby Layne feels utterly and completely alone, though she is not. I am very near, feeling utterly and completely helpless as I watch the scene unfold. You can't imagine how terrible it is for me to be present and not be allowed to do more. I have been part of her life for so many years, helping and guiding her, without her being aware of my identity. Why can't this be the time I make my presence known, reveal that there are other angels here too? Why must I wait? Why can't I stop what is happening? I don't understand.

But only the Power greater than angels is wise enough to answer these questions and understand the meaning of this moment. That same Power is also present and will provide the help that is most needed.

As I finally accept the fact that there will be no rescue, a strange calm settles over me. I become aware I am observing the situation as if from another person's eyes. It is to *me* this is happening, but I am also watching from outside my physical body. Time becomes irrelevant; has a second, a minute, an hour or a year passed? I have no conception of time or space. I am suspended in someone else's nightmare.

Toward the end of the tall wooden fence which runs parallel to the street and the back of a large yard, we pass a short set of steps leading up to a latch-gate. It is up these steps and through this gate I am dragged, finally struggling to get away since no help has come. But the man is too strong. I am aware now that my own worst fear is about to happen to me.

I offer up a prayer and vow to myself, "I will come out of this alive." Even as I am being raped, I continue talking and talking, though I have no idea what I'm saying. At the same time I am praying. If I raise my voice, even speaking, he menacingly grabs my throat. Though I am not being beaten, I surmise that if I antagonize him, he might become even more violent. His breath smells of alcohol; my best hope is to remain as calm as possible and attempt to calm him with my constant chatter. There is a certainty that if I scream or struggle he will kill me. I am determined to come out of this alive.

In some strange way, I must have mesmerized the man, because as he leaves me, taking my watch and ring, there is no move to do me any further harm. Instead of my walking out of the gate immediately, I suggest that he might want to go first to get away; I *don't* want him behind me. Can you imagine? I am telling my rapist how to make his getaway!! It is as though someone else has written a bizarre script which we both are following, regardless of the fact that it makes absolutely no sense. He never argues and does as I suggest, walking calmly through the gate, then running up the street.

As soon as he is out of sight, I pass through the gate and run to the nearest house. Not until this moment does my composure completely disintegrate. I break down and sob. I knock on the door and am greeted by a woman I don't know.

"I have just been raped. May I use your phone to call the police?"

Just saying those words hurls me back into that state of detachment I experienced during my ordeal. The woman is kind and somewhat at a loss for words as we wait for the police to arrive. In a world of suspended animation, I calmly give the woman officer a full description of what has happened.

I am taken to the hospital by the police. The tests to which I am subjected and the questions I am asked are humiliating, but I am treated with respect and kindness. I wonder if everyone who cries "Rape" is treated as well. I suspect that many are not. After all, I am married to a doctor and live on the "nice" side of town.

Harry is called and comes to the hospital, having no idea what has happened, only that I have been taken there for some reason. Seeing the nurses' faces as he arrives, he expects the worst. He is so happy to see me *alive,* that when I tell him what has actually happened, his reaction is one of tremendous relief. In fact, I feel a little hurt that he seems to take it so calmly. Doesn't he know what I've been through?

Harry drives me to the police station where I work with a police artist putting together a composite drawing of my attacker. This presents no problem. I had stared at his face, looked him directly in the eye for however long we were together. I know *exactly* what he looks like. The picture will appear in the paper the next day.

We return home, where, for the rest of the day, the phone never stops ringing and people continue to drop by. In our small city, news of an event such as this travels quickly. I am able to talk about my experience and remain in that strange state of surrealism I felt earlier. I sit down in my study and write a detailed description of everything I can remember of the rape, from beginning to end. Completely exhausted after the longest day of my life, I finally, with medication, fall asleep, curled up safely in the arms of my husband.

During the next week, family and friends visit, call or write. It is an awkward situation for everyone. No one knows quite what to say or do, but each wants to help in some way. I take it upon myself to make *them* feel more comfortable, more at ease. This event has a dramatic effect on them too. Someone they know has been assaulted on a safe street in the middle of the day. It makes everyone realize that it could happen to them, and they are afraid. I am afraid. The man is still out there.

Many times when a woman is raped, she isolates herself and doesn't want to be out in public for awhile. I choose instead, to go on with my life. On Monday, I return to work at school. There and everywhere else, I talk freely about my experience. I encourage my students to voice their concerns and honestly answer their questions about an event most had only associated with movies or TV.

My family is somewhat worried I am handling the rape a little *too* well. They are concerned that I am not being honest with myself, not facing my true feelings and fears. I wonder, too, why this horrendous experience hasn't affected me as deeply as it might. I give myself permission to totally fall apart, if need be. I give myself permission to *not* be strong, to *not* be brave. I promise to allow myself anything needed to recover from this terrible event.

Several mornings after the rape, I wake up in my bed. Harry has gone to work, and I am alone. I sit bolt upright, feeling an energy inside my body like lava smoldering in a dormant volcano. From deep within me the energy begins building, building, rising steadily upward until I can contain it no longer. The explosion erupts in a hot flow of pent-up anguish. The horror of what I have experienced and the fears that still plague me come bubbling to the surface of my conscious mind and overflow in a torrent of tears and screams. This cleansing session lasts for quite some time. Later, feeling much relieved, I vow to allow any such outburst in the future if needed.

But for me, talking to friends and family seems the most natural and effective process to my recovery. Harry is supportive, loving and doesn't react in the negative way some husbands do in this situation.

The family in which I grew up had always been able to bring humor to any situation, even the worst. In the newspaper the week after my rape there is an article reporting that it is "Rape Awareness Week." As I relate this to my sister she chastises me saying, "Oh, Libby Layne, you do tend to overdo getting involved in things don't you?"

Her familiar humor aids in my recovery.

In the days following, I learn of the sincere love and concern people in the community have for me. Old friends, acquaintances and even strangers express their genuine interest in my experience. They send flowers, write notes, come by for a hug or to drop off food they have made. They pray for me daily, and I am surrounded by a network of compassion and support.

There are other friends who have a different reaction to my experience, offering a different perspective. It is their view that we all *choose* the lessons with which we are confronted in life, in order to grow. On some level this may be true. Yet, in my situation, this belief seemed to give them license to offer me no sympathy, empathy or understanding for the pain and fear I feel following the rape. If I *chose* it, I could deal with it myself, seemed to be their attitude. I come to realize that whether I choose my own fate, or whether it is chosen *for* me or *with* me by a Higher Power, or whether I am completely at the mercy of fate itself, I need compassion in my pain. No matter how strong I appear on the outside, I want to be offered a shoulder to cry on, to hear, "It's all right Libby, you'll be fine, I'm here."

One phrase I hear frequently from everyone who knows me is, "If anyone can get over something like this, you can."

For years I have believed this about myself, yet there is a gnawing doubt lurking under the surface. My life, other than the normal hurts of human existence, has been blessed. My attitude is positive, my faith solid. But am I only a fake Pollyanna? How will I bear up now that something really terrible has happened? Will I *really* get over this?

At the school during the next week, police photos are brought for me to view. I am positive I can identify him, but each time I look at the faces in the book, I am less sure. What if I identify the wrong man?

Finally, I see the face. "That's him, I'm sure."

Yet I continue on to the end of the book. Suddenly, I see another man I recognize. Reticent, I point and say, "That looks like him too." I am beginning to doubt my judgement. This man has glasses; my attacker had worn sunglasses. But what about the other man I identified in the picture before?

The detective smiles broadly. "They are the same man. You identified him first *without* his glasses."

An officer at the police station recognizes the man in the composite drawing we had done and put a name to it. The man has a long record and is out on parole. A few days later he is arrested. He has given his name and address to the pawn shop where he took my watch and ring — not a brilliant move! But perhaps he was thinking that a woman in this part of town will not report a rape because of the stigma attached. Was he ever wrong! He may have been "watching me" but he did not know me!

The attitude I formed about rape in general, before it happened to me, is a primary factor in how I react to it afterwards. I believe rape to be an act of violence by someone who wants power over someone else. A woman has no cause to feel disgraced, as it has nothing to do with anything she does or doesn't do. She is a victim as any other victim of violence. I do remember that during my whole ordeal, it was important to me that I hold my head off the ground and look him in the eye. I was never completely in his power. My head was held as high as was humanly possible.

Another reason for my recovery is my philosophy that something positive can come out of even the worst circumstance. My present situation is a real test of that philosophy. I can choose to continue to be a victim for the rest of my life, or see it as an isolated event. I find it completely natural to choose the latter. My belief is holding and being strengthened. This one event will not destroy me as it has so many women; I choose to move forward.

All of these — family, friends, humor, attitude, and a strong sense of self — see me through my ordeal. But, without question, I know my spiritual faith is the most important factor in my recovery. Throughout, I am aware of an abiding "Grace" enfolding me like a soft blanket. I had prayed during the rape, and I continue to pray constantly when I feel afraid or confused. I am even able to come to a place of forgiveness for the man who raped me.

I use this time to review my beliefs about God, Grace and why things like this happen to people. I have never believed it to be God's will that tragedies occur. It would make no sense that a loving Creator would *will* his creation to suffer. The imperfect world in which humans live, however, is filled with tragic, unexpected events. For me, it is how we react to these events that makes the difference. With God's help, we can choose to be positive or negative in our response. This does not mean in the process there will be no suffering; this is the human condition, for the present. To support us in this condition, I believe a spiritual force called "Grace" is available for the asking. This force, as I experienced it, is a key in the healing process. Certainly there are many factors that enter into my recovery. I believe its speed and completeness could not have occurred without God's abiding Grace.

Because we have such overwhelming evidence against the man who raped me, both my lawyer and his, hope for a quick plea bargain. But my rapist will have none of it. Does he think I will back down or not want to testify? Whatever the reason, we go to trial in February of the next year.

As I sit waiting to testify before a judge at the grand jury, a doubt crosses my mind. "When he walks in the courtroom, what if I am uncertain he is *really* the man?"

As positive as I had been when I identified his picture in the police files, I am gripped by the fear that I may have made a mistake. Except for that picture I have not seen the man since September.

The door opens and a handcuffed man is led into the courtroom by a uniformed officer. I turn to look at him and catch his eyes also looking for me. Our eyes lock. There is no doubt; *this* is the man. From that point on I am totally confident and the perfect witness. Having been on stage for years, I am at ease and relate the details of my rape in a straightforward, articulate manner.

When I finish, the judge asks me, "Do you see the man in this courtroom?"

Without the shadow of a doubt, I look the man directly in the eye and point to him saying, "*That* is the man." He is sentenced to eighty-nine years.

I am asked to be interviewed for an article in the newspaper. It is a common practice at this time to withhold the name of a rape victim in the media. Though there has been publicity about the rape, my name has not been printed or mentioned. Agreeing to do the article, I initially ask that my name not be used. As I am being interviewed, however, the reporter comments that my attitude is quite unusual and positive; other women could benefit from hearing it. Almost at the same moment we realize how much stronger this statement would be if I allow the reporter to use my name. And why not? There is nothing for which I am ashamed.

The article appears on the front page of the Sunday paper beside a color picture of me, defiantly shaking my hand as I emphasize some point I am making. In the story, I explain my attitude toward rape and my choice not to remain a victim.

Letters pour in from women throughout the area who have been raped and want to feel as I do about their experience. Everyone agrees this is a message that is long past due. I speak at a local women's college and am asked to be a part of Rape Companions, a local crisis service for women who have been raped.

Though I now have great compassion for other women who have been raped, I don't feel called to be a crusader in this field. I occasionally talk with those sent by others who believe I might be of help but choose to treat this experience as an isolated event in my life, not as the center of it. In other areas of the country, women who have been raped are expressing attitudes similar to mine and are also doing articles and interviews. This crusade can be led by others. For me, there is another path, other causes for which I am being prepared. If only someone would tell me what they are!

I am so proud of the way Libby Layne handled her rape experience and that she accepted the help she was offered by God. She also became more aware of other realms of reality. As she remembers that day, she feels that she was not alone. She doesn't know yet that I was there. I am still an "angel, unaware."

She is wondering for what she is being prepared. It is so tempting to just tell her everything, but I won't. I must continue to guide her to new pieces of her puzzle and help her to recognize them. The closer she gets, the more excited I become.

Spring, 1989

At the school, I am moving both physically and emotionally away from my involvement as I watch the school move farther away from my idea of the original vision. I am preparing the students and the administration for what I now realize will be my retirement from the school this fall. The students are disappointed. I assure them there will certainly be another music teacher when I leave and I will come to visit often.

I continue exploring the world of sound therapy and develop an innovative system for changing classes using carefully programed music and a timing system. Called, "Music on Time," this system signals the change of classes not with an irritating bell or buzzer, but the music of harps, crystal bowls and music which promotes relaxation and concentration. It is quite a hit with students and teachers alike.

I find myself also being drawn back to my interest in special children. Though the students at the school have special needs, it is not the same. I realize there will never be a place here for the little ones with whom I feel such a bond. I learn of a five-year-old boy with Down's Syndrome who loves music and whose mother wants to encourage this interest. Chris begins coming after school, and I work and play with him in my music room. He sits with his little legs dangling from a large stool and exuberantly plays a drum set I have brought. When I play an orchestral selection on the recorder, he is the conductor. The height of the session and his favorite activity is the playing of the "flying" theme song from the movie *ET*. As the music soars, Chris raises his tiny arms in the air toward me and with a broad smile begs, "Fly me Libby. Fly me like ET."

I place him face down atop my arms, and as I twirl him in a circle, we soar together "across the moon" in a magical world of music and make-believe!

The joy that I feel lets me know I am back on my path. It feels *right* again. My passion returns, and I look with excitement and confidence to both endings and beginnings.

VII
Theme and Variations I

Thou wilt keep him in perfect peace, whose mind is staid on Thee.
In Him is no darkness at all.
The darkness and the light to Him are all the same.
(from a setting of Psalm 139 by S.S.Wesley)

September, 1989

The ordeal of last September has left me with an assurance of the relevance of my present spiritual beliefs, yet a desire to explore new territory. There is something mystical about how my body and soul are healing. I recall the experience of leaving my body at the moment of my rape and remember the presence of "others." In this past year, I have noticed a heightened sense of everything around me and a keener insight.

From time to time in the past I have felt a need for more of the mystical in my spiritual life. Little was taught in the church of my youth about the mysterious side of God and Jesus. There were, of course, stories of burning bushes, seas parting, angel visitations and Jesus's miracles. These seemed to be happenings related to the Bible of ancient times, never to the present day or to average people. Grown-up Christians I knew accepted these unbelievable tales on "faith," many afraid to doubt their literal truth. We children, on the other hand, had no problem with the miraculous. We had a way of seeing the real Truth found in a story. I suppose this is what Jesus meant when He said we must "become as little children" to enter His kingdom.

As I grow older I question the miracle stories and the mysterious happenings in the Bible. I never lose my faith, but it is no longer important to me whether or not these stories are absolutely true. Still, there is a part of me that longs for my experience as a little child, a desire for belief in the miraculous.

This has led me to an interest in New Age philosophy. On the surface it seems to offer much of what I have been seeking. The reading I do and the people I meet during this phase of my spiritual journey accept Jesus as Son of God, but in a new and different way.

I am cautious on this exploratory trip into the world of metaphysics. Having been taught in my youth of a sometimes vengeful and jealous God, I always worry of His judgement in the event I create my own "Golden Calf." I carry into my adulthood an almost paranoid fear of being punished for believing the *wrong thing*. Each time I go off on a tangent in my search, a little voice says, "Are you getting too far away from your Christian roots?" Believing that I was born into the Christian faith for a good reason, I am very careful as I go on my spiritual excursions.

I am warned by other well-meaning Christians that I am in dangerous territory. Some even say that New Age is a plot by the Devil to overthrow Christianity. I know they are concerned about my welfare and assure them that I am both prayerful and discerning in this exploration. I trust that the spirit within me will guide me to the Truth.

I enjoy the freedom of thought offered by the metaphysical approach to explaining how the Universe works. I am delighted meeting many people who are grounded spiritually in other religious traditions and are also searching for Truth. I love the *idea* of reincarnation, though I am not sure it is exactly the way humans have envisioned it. As I am introduced to other and varied beliefs, I keep an open mind, joining discussion groups, going to conferences and experimenting with different kinds of meditation and prayer. To my delight, the dolphins turn up again in my reading. They are held in high esteem by followers of the New Age Movement. Theories abound as to why they may have been created, and many believe they have special powers of healing and teaching. I take in all of this with great interest and a healthy "grain of salt." I am becoming aware that the dolphins keep reappearing periodically throughout my life's journey, and I wonder whether there is some reason for it.

As taken as I am with these new ideas, there are a few things in particular that keep me from accepting fully the New Age package.

The first is the whole phenomenon of "channelers." These are people who believe that teacher guides from other dimensions communicate great truths through them. Followers from all over the country come to listen to these channelers and hang on every word. This is a bit too weird, even for me. My belief is that I am, indeed, guided by a spirit within me which I call the Holy Spirit. Why would I need strange speaking spirits, taking over other people's bodies, minds, and voices, to impart spiritual truths to me? Many of these channelers, though not all, are misusing their spiritual gifts to gain power and money. Unfortunately this can happen in religions or philosophies when the real truth gets mixed up in human failings. The abuses of the Christian church throughout history have shown that any truth can be used in a negative way. In fact, many people drawn to the New Age Movement were hurt in the past by the traditional church and church people. Their spiritual needs not being met, they leave, looking for truth elsewhere.

Another New Age belief that troubles me encourages the view that humans are Divine because God is within them. There are those who use the expression, "I am God." This doesn't ring true to me. Though I believe we are created in God's image, that a spark of the divine dwells in each of us, the idea that *at this moment* we are exactly the *same* as God is one I cannot accept.

I begin to develop a new perspective on miracles, healing, and angels from my reading, and although I don't embrace everything I read, hear or even everything I experience, I take a fresh look at the miracles and mysteries of the Bible. During this phase of my spiritual journey, my understanding of Jesus is deepened. I look for new ways of viewing His Sonship of God, His mission on earth and the truth of what that means. I wonder if the truth I have found in New Age teachings can be harmonized with the Truth in my Christianity. Could my experiences of the mystical be accepted within the traditional church in which I wish to remain?

And just where *is* the mystery, where *are* the healings in modern Christianity? According to Jesus's promise, His followers would do not only what He had done, but even more. Paul speaks of being "out of body." Was that different from the "out of body" experienced by some in meditation at the conferences I attended? St. John explains in his Gospel that Jesus, The Word, was there at the creation of everything and is part of everything created. Wasn't that what these people were saying about everything being ONE? What was the difference between psychic experiences, telepathy and Jesus *knowing* about the five husbands of the woman at the well? So much of what I am learning and experiencing makes my Christianity more real to me. Yet, there are still nagging doubts about the New Age Movement, and I am not willing to leave my path as a Christian.

I ask for guidance and wait.

I receive a brochure in the mail announcing a meeting in Washington D.C. for mental health professionals and counselors. It will explore the importance of counselors understanding connections between spiritual and mental health. As I read through the list of various speakers attending, I see the title, "Rediscovering the Mystical in Christianity."

A Carmelite Monk, says the brochure, will teach a seminar discussing the loss of the mystical in the Christian church. She will be exploring why New Age and metaphysical principles have become so popular and how they relate to basic Christian beliefs.

I immediately sign up for the conference.

On the first day of the seminar, I enter a room packed with people excitedly talking. Obviously, I am not the only one interested in this subject. Everyone is asked to take a seat, and the speaker is introduced.

"This is Mother Tessa," says a young man.

Into the room walks a tiny, beautiful girl of about 28. She is dressed in a long brown monk's robe with a rope belt. On her feet are what I call "Jesus sandals." Her dark brown hair is tied back in a brown kerchief and reaches almost to her waist. Her step is lively and her smile mischievous. As she begins her talk, there is no mistaking; this monk is no stodgy prudish cleric.

"If it is difficult for you to call me a monk instead of a nun you may think of me as a 'nunk,'" she says.

Everyone is immediately captivated by this charming woman, and as she continues, I know this is what I have come to hear. Everything falls into place, as Mother Tessa explains how the mysterious or mystical tradition, existing during Jesus's time and accepted by early Christians, has somehow become lost. Through the years, many factors have played a part in the elimination of this essential part of Christianity — the Age of Reason, the Scientific Revolution, even the Church itself. Christians today, living in a violent and confusing world, are looking for answers which they are not finding in rigid beliefs and religious dogma. Somewhere inside, they know there is more. This is why, she says, the New Age Movement has grown so dramatically during the past few years. She does not insinuate that it is evil or even wrong, but she believes that the answers they seek are all contained within the Christian tradition. It is simply a matter of rediscovering what has been lost.

She introduces the audience to early Christian mystics: St. John of the Cross, St. Ignatius, Meister Eckhert and others. Most interesting to me are the eleventh and twelfth century women mystics: Hildegard of Bingen, Julian of Norwich, Mechtild of Magdeburg and the woman after whom Mother Tessa is named, Teresa of Avila. These Christian women were having mystical experiences and writing literature about God abiding in all things centuries ago. There are striking similarities to New Age thought, yet by putting the mystical into a Christian context, I find the comfort level I have been seeking. This is not a new and trendy philosophy, but ancient Christian tradition. My long-held fear that I was straying is replaced by a certainty; by having the courage and faith to explore, I now have a greater understanding of my Christianity. Literature written by early Christian mystics leads me to a new understanding in my rereading of the Bible.

Interested in learning more of the contemplative life and Christian meditation, I sign up to make a week-long retreat next May at the Carmelite Monastery in Nova Scotia with the monks and "nunks."

I wonder whether this has any connection to autistic children and dolphins. I can see no obvious link as yet, but I have learned that anything that captures my interest to this extent is bound to be part of this puzzle I seem to be working.

The lessons she is learning about her Christianity will be an important part of her understanding of the dolphins and her work with the autistic children. Are you beginning to see how things fit together like a puzzle? Can you begin to understand how life can be an adventure when you follow your soul's path as it leads you forward?

Libby Layne is becoming more aware of the puzzle she is putting together, and actively looking for the pieces. The picture on the box top is still hidden as it is meant to be.

Now, right on schedule, it's time for those dolphins to appear in her life again.

Virginia Beach, April, 1990

As I walk along the oceanfront, I see a pod of dolphins swimming far offshore. It is early in the morning, with only a few people on the beach.

I have never been near a dolphin, though my fascination with them is now over twenty years old. Knowing the possibility of their telepathic ability, I decide to "will" them closer. In my mind, I formulate an invitation, asking the dolphins to come meet me. I incorporate praying in the spirit, a type of prayer I experienced during my Bible study days.

As I continue along, concentrating intently on my mission, I notice people pointing excitedly at the water, just where the waves are breaking. I look, and there in the water, following me as I walk, is one lone Bottlenose Dolphin. He has chosen to leave his pod as they continue on their way without him.

Since I am quite certain he has answered my invitation, it is only polite that I acknowledge his arrival by greeting him in the water. Watching as this scene unfolds is a woman standing on the beach. I explain to her that this dolphin has come at my request.

"Would you please hold my watch and ring while I go in?" I ask, having never seen the woman before.

Though she could well have walked away with my jewelry, it was a chance I was willing to take at this auspicious moment. She appeared to be honest, interested only in the rather odd proceedings.

I enter the water where I last saw the dolphin. I am wearing no life preserver, and though a strong swimmer, I quickly begin to tire as the waves break over me again and again. I can no longer see the dolphin, but sense his presence hovering in the water. For years I have waited for this moment. Yet, perceiving the formidable size of this creature, I become fearful.

I have no idea how long I have stayed in the water; time is suspended. Breathless and exhausted, I finally go ashore. Those who have gathered for the show, tell me they saw the dolphin beside me, though he did not come to the surface. I wonder if he sensed my fear.

Retrieving my watch and ring from the honest bystander, I continue my walk down the beach. The dolphin still swims along the shoreline in the same direction. It appears he is following me. I hesitate to turn around, certain he will leave me and return to his pod. If I remain on this course however, I will soon be in North Carolina! I decide it wise to go back the other way. Ready to say good-bye to my new friend, I resume my walk in the other direction. To my utter amazement, the dolphin also turns, following me back up the beach until I reach my motel. As I offer my thanks to him and walk off the beach, he swims out to sea, rejoining his pod in the deep waters of the Atlantic.

My first dolphin encounter has been brief and a bit frightening. Yet its enticement is enough to know dolphins are in my life to stay. I look forward to the upcoming summer when my family rents a house right on the oceanfront for two weeks. I'm beginning to be suspicious that the dolphin connection in my life has some special meaning, that there is a plan associated with it.

Why haven't I been told what it is?

Why indeed?! I sometimes wonder the same thing myself. At least she's beginning to realize there must be a larger plan for the dolphins in her life than just for entertainment. That's a start. The interlude with the dolphin stimulates her appetite for new experiences, new adventures.

Psalm 46 — Revisited
Be still and know that I am God

From her beginnings she was seldom still
And she knew God
A large noisy family bustled with activity
And she knew God
From morning 'til night never stopping
And she knew God

A trip to the north where monks prayed
In Solitude
Everyone laughed
You....quiet?

In a hermitage named Elizabeth
She cooked and cleaned
In Silence
She walked and ate
In Silence
And she knew God
In the Silence

But one day
In a hermitage named Elizabeth
She sang and danced
To the music of the Supremes
And she knew God
In the Noise
Doesn't really matter, does it?
God is in Both.

May, 1990

I recognize the brown habit as the "nunk" asks, "Are you Elizabeth?"

From the airport in Kemptville, Nova Scotia, we take a large farm truck, laden with supplies, to the Nova Nada Monastery an hour away. Nada means "nothing" and that pretty much describes what I first encounter on my first monastic retreat. Yet isn't it for this I have come — solitude?

The setting is a natural paradise with mammoth evergreens surrounding a still partially frozen lake. Dotted around the property are tiny log cabins in which retreatants stay alone. There is a beautiful library and a chapel which are always open. A large building called "Elias" is the dining hall where there will be only one meal with other retreatants and the community of monks.

I have happened by chance upon a week of *complete solitude*. We are to maintain a strict silence, speaking to no one unless absolutely necessary.

Complete silence? No idle conversation? No theological chats over herbal tea? No sharing the experience? What have I gotten myself into?

I am assigned a spiritual friend who will be there if I wish to discuss something important. The "nunk" I had heard at the conference, Mother Tessa, is now at their monastery in Colorado. I am disappointed, as I had hoped to come to know her better.

I am taken to the supply rooms in Elias where I pick up the food which I will cook and eat alone in my hermitage. There will be morning and evening prayer in community, and we can work in the garden or the kitchen, helping with meals. Even in these situations, there is to be no idle chatter. This is going to be a challenge!

Brother Tom shows me to my hermitage. On a rough wooden sign above the door is carved the name "Elizabeth."

"We thought you might feel comfortable here. It is named after a Carmelite nun, Elizabeth of the Trinity."

I am touched by the sentiment and fascinated anew at yet another one of those so-called coincidences which again and again appear in my life.

Settled in my snug little hermitage named Elizabeth, I face seven twenty-four hour days of unstructured solitude. There are no lists of errands, no telephone calls to make, no good deeds to do. What in the world am I going to do with all that time?

The hermitage has the odor of burning wood and the musty smell of an old cabin on the river where we went as children. There is a black potbellied stove in the center of the room, the sole source of heat. Though it is May, spring is still just a hope. The stove is also used for cooking. I am told where I can chop my wood to keep the fire going. The room has a sofa, several over-stuffed chairs and a table with only an oil lamp for light. Upstairs in the tiny loft, looking out over the lake, is the bed where I will sleep. On it are piled tattered quilts and blankets. Under these, other seekers, such as I, have cuddled for warmth as the fire downstairs has burned out by morning. I am fortunate; I have an indoor toilet. My one modern convenience.

Each morning I wake, shivering as I put fresh logs on the fire. The day starts at 5:30 AM when I prepare to go to the chapel for 6:00 o'clock morning prayer. Following this I make my breakfast. If I have cereal, I also mix dry milk; there is no refrigeration. I wash my dishes in water fetched in a bucket from the stream and warmed on the stove. This takes me only to 7:00 AM! The rest of the day stretches like an endless void ahead of me. I have certain choices: I can take walks, read, pray, go to the library, take walks, go to the library, pray, read, and, oh yes, I can work in the garden with the "nunks." I don't *ever* work in the yard at home, so this is not an appealing choice for me. I had expectations of *some* solitude, but I also had visions of long spiritual discussions with the monks there. I am not sure this is at all what I had in mind.

It *is,* however, what God has in mind.

As the week progresses, I become aware that each task I perform becomes a holy one; opening a can of beans, chopping firewood, washing dishes or lighting the oil lamp are all consecrated acts. I am aware of every second and in that second am intensely aware of what I am doing. Each moment is sacred as the silence becomes full of the sounds of everyday existence. It is a symphony of the simple, a concerto of the ordinary. The music fills me with its melody until I can stand it no longer. I go for a walk where no one can hear me and sing all the hymns of praise of my youth to the trees, to the sky, and with the birds. I become Julie Andrews in *The Sound of Music,* as I sing "The hills are alive" with an abandoned vibrato!

During the week, I speak briefly with Sister Pat, the spiritual friend to whom I have been assigned. I listen to audiotapes giving spiritual direction in subjects relating to the Carmelite Order. At Morning Prayer I hear a prayer to which I am particularly drawn. When I inquire about its author, I learn it was written by Elizabeth of the Trinity after whom my hermitage is named. I ask for a copy and begin praying it aloud everyday. I study contemplative prayer techniques at which I am particularly unsuited. Extended periods of silence seem to cause my mind to behave like a popcorn machine, with kernels of thoughts forever exploding into what is supposed to be tranquil meditation.

I offer my skills in the dining hall kitchen where I *silently* make a huge pot of my favorite soup. I even resort to an afternoon of *silent* hoeing and weed-pulling in the vegetable garden alongside *silent,* brown-habited, Jesus-sandaled monks.

At the end of the week I have one final meal with the other retreatants and monks there. It is good to communicate with language again, and I realize that though this has been a good exercise, I was never meant to be a "nunk." The last day, ready for my imminent return to civilization, I go to the library. They have a good selection of cassette tapes, both study tapes and music. There, for some reason, is an old tape of the Supremes. I check it out, go back to Hermitage Elizabeth, and put the tape in my recorder. I turn it on full blast, and the music fills the room. With the familiar hand choreography at the appropriate lines, I joyfully lift my voice up to the rafters of that little hermitage, singing, "Stop in the Name of Love!" I'm sure the angels joined me in my song of praise!

You bet we did! It was quite an occasion. Of course it isn't one of my usual songs of praise, but when the spirit moves the heart, the style of the song makes no difference. It's the expressing of joy that is important.

July, 1990

Summer has come in Virginia, and it is time for our yearly family gathering. For twenty-odd years, Harry and I have spent one or two weeks with our children at the beach. In recent years we began inviting my parents, my sisters, their husbands and children. My parents are not fond of the beach but enjoy seeing everyone together. It is a time when the California cousins visit and become better acquainted with their Virginia cousins. Love and laughter abound, and we all cherish this special time together.

I am particularly excited this year. After my mini-experience in May, I am anxious for a *real* dolphin encounter. I am positive that the dolphin I saw then is out there waiting for me, this time with his family and friends. The house we are renting is a large, old-style beach house with white shingle siding, green shutters, and a huge porch that stretches across the front. It is not plush but is comfortable and spacious with ample room for everyone. My favorite feature is the large grassy front yard which overlooks the beach front; it is here I set up my dolphin watch.

Every morning I get up, eat a light breakfast, put on my bathing suit and suntan lotion, pick up my life preserver, walk to the wooden chair on the lawn, and seat myself facing the ocean. From here I am able to view the expanse of beach from north to south as I wait for the dolphins to swim by. Early morning and late afternoon are best. At the first sight of them in the distance, I race down to the beach, donning my life preserver on the run. Meeting the oncoming waves, I splash into the surf, swimming as fast as I can to cross the path of the dolphins. I am *always* late. By the time I get there, they have swum by, never knowing what they missed! I swim back to shore, trudge back to the beach house, rinse off the sand and salt, reapply lotion and again take up my vigil on the lawn chair.

Day after day I perform this ritual, hopefully waiting for an exciting encounter. There are days I don't see a single dolphin, but I am determined. That dolphin who came to visit me in May is out there, and I want to see him again!

In my family there is a history of good-natured teasing, and my dolphin watch is a situation crying for a good rib. The most vocal is my father, who is enjoying this immensely. "Libby Layne, these are wild animals; they aren't going to pay any attention to you."

As the two weeks come to an end, even the teasing ceases as everyone begins to feel a little sorry for me. I have been sitting in that chair for twelve days, running down to the beach, swimming into the water, and haven't once been *near* a dolphin.

I learn as the days go by that timing is the most important factor. If I see them coming, I must get in their path *before* they pass.

On the day before everyone is scheduled to leave, I take my post in my chair on the lawn, gazing out over the ocean. I see a large pod coming far up the beach, but close in to the shore. Racing to the edge of the water as I put on my little red life preserver, I swim out into the path of the dolphins, and today my timing is perfect! I find myself totally surrounded by thirty dolphins! At this moment I realize how large these mammals are, and I am a bit frightened. Their sleek grey bodies glide effortlessly through the water, circling around my body, covered only with a bathing suit and a tiny life preserver. I suppose it is that built-in grin on their faces that gives us the idea they wouldn't hurt a flea.

I become comfortable in their presence, assuming for some reason that I was meant to be here. I begin making different sounds, toning, Om sounds, and overtone chanting. I don't reach to touch them or get too near them, waiting for them to take the lead. The sounds I make seem to interest the dolphins as they stay in close proximity to me in the water. This would be considered a real "dolphin encounter," one in which both *human* and *dolphin* are aware of the other and the dolphin chooses to interact with the human. The dolphins are very curious about this strange creature making strange sounds. One lone dolphin swims up to me, faces me and gives me his undivided attention. I am not afraid, but am in awe of this incredible moment. Suddenly he dives deeply into the ocean, and I say to myself, "He's going to come up under me and flip me over." Instead, he leaps high out of the water, does a complete flip and splashes down right in front of me. It is almost like a salute as he comes flying out of the water. Immediately, several of the others join him in a synchronized leap just for me.

In captivity, dolphins are trained to do this as a trick for a show. When they do it in the wild, they are expressing joy or excitement. The dolphins stay for a short time longer, then move on, bored with this creature who is unable to return their salute.

Swimming happily back to shore, I am greeted by a crowd that has gathered. Everyone is excited, especially my family.

Inside, Daddy gives me a sheepish grin, saying, "I wish I hadn't seen that."

Actually he is quite pleased, but mostly relieved. Not being a strong swimmer and never having swum in the ocean, his teasing has also come from a sincere concern for my safety.

The next summer I am joined by my two sisters, my two daughters and the California cousins for many wonderful encounters. Our success is in part due to the lessons learned last summer about timing our arrival in the dolphins' path. We go out in rafts, inner tubes and life preservers, waiting until we are right in the middle of the swimming pod. Since the dolphins had been interested in sounds last year, my sisters and I sing three part harmony to them. Our aquatic arrangement of the spiritual *Do Lord,* is a particular favorite, sung to the words, "Do Dolphin, Do Dolphin, Do Remember Me!" They stay around even more this year, and no one makes fun of me or my impossible dream again. I have made the dream come true.

There's that spirit of tenacity again. She just doesn't give up easily when she makes up her mind about something.

Now it's time for Libby Layne to find another piece of her puzzle. This one will be an especially important clue in solving the mystery of the Sound of the Dolphin's Psalm.

VIII
Chorale and Fugue

September, 1990

While in the store ordering a book about autism, the clerk asks, "Have you heard of *The Sound of a Miracle?* I know it's about a girl with autism, but I don't know anything else."

"Order it, please!" I reply immediately. Autism and sound have been mentioned in the same book. This is definitely something I need to look into.

I have wondered if there were some connection between my interest in dolphins, autism, and sound therapy. If there were, what would that mean for my future? Is the reading and research I have done only for my entertainment or does it have a special meaning? I have sensed something or someone guiding me in this search, but for what reason?

The Sound of a Miracle, by Annabel Stehli, is a mother's story of her discovery of a treatment for her autistic daughter called Audio-Integration Therapy. This treatment is based on the findings of Dr. Alfred Tomatis, a French ENT physician. Dr. Tomatis learned from his medical practice that proper listening by the human ear has great importance to the workings of a healthy brain. He developed a method whereby he used high and low frequency sounds to retrain the ear for better listening skills. He observed positive results after using this method with some individuals who stuttered, had dyslexia, or autism. From Dr. Tomatis's method, another French physician, Dr. Guy Berard, has developed Audio-Enhancement-Training. It was this physician who had treated Georgie, the girl in *The Sound of a Miracle.*

For Georgie, who had been diagnosed for twelve years with autism, sound was a key factor in her recovery from autistic symptoms. She, as many with autism, was hypersensitive or overly sensitive to certain sounds — sounds that are inaudible to most people.

The sound of water running through a pipe somewhere in the house, for instance, was, to her ears, a tidal wave. By using an audio test, it was determined to which sound frequencies Georgie was most sensitive. These frequencies were played through earphones for a certain number of sessions, retraining her hearing mechanism and resulting in her eventual escape from the confusing world of autism. Now able to function in the world, Georgie went on to earn her PhD and now helps others with autism. Her parents were so impressed with the method, they brought it to the United States. After the book, *The Sound of a Miracle,* was published, the demand for the treatment from other parents was astounding. Professionals were skeptical, but eventually were forced to look at the positive results.

What really excites me is the use of high and low frequency sounds as a treatment. Moreover, the positive results being observed are identical to those Dr. Betsy Smith had seen in her study twenty years before — her study of *people with autism swimming with the dolphins!* I begin my pacing routine. Would it not stand to reason, if sound were a major factor in some autistics' improvement with AIT, that dolphin sounds, which range from very low to very high frequency, could also be a factor in Dr. Smith's study?

If I examine the dolphin sounds from a scientific approach, I recall that recorded dolphin sounds range from whistles, which lie in the 6,000-18,000 hertz range, to echo location sounds in the 2,000 to 6,000 hertz range. Humans can hear sounds within a range of frequencies from about 20 hertz to about 17,000 hertz. It has been found that when two or more frequencies are emitted together, other frequency sound waves are produced as a result. This means a tremendous variety of frequency waves may be produced when the dolphin sounds are recorded.

In reading about the many effects of sound, I had been intrigued by a phenomenon called "entrainment." As explained by Don Campbell in his book *Music, Physician for Times to Come*, entrainment occurs when the strong vibrations of one object cause another object, vibrating at a weaker rate, to lock into and vibrate at the rate of the first object. This is best illustrated when a tuning fork vibrating at a certain frequency or speed is brought into close proximity of another tuning fork. Without touching the second tuning fork, the first can set up a vibration in the second. The more harmonically related the two forks are, the more entrainment or sympathetic vibration takes place.

Experts in the field of sound have studied this phenomenon as it related to how brain wave patterns can be altered by certain vibratory frequencies. Could the multifrequency sounds of the recorded dolphin communications somehow be "entraining" and calming the distorted brain wave patterns of the autistic children? Were their brain wave vibrations "harmonically related" to the dolphin sounds? I still feel there is more.

I am making a connection that brings together all three of my passionate interests. Am I really putting something together, or am I trying too hard to make the pieces fit? In my desire to find meaning in everything, am I taking all this and myself too seriously? It really makes no difference, I'll still follow this lead to its conclusion. It's what makes my life an adventure.

February, 1991

As soon as I read the article in the airplane magazine, I know that I will go, even though it means cancelling my return trip to the Monastery in Nova Scotia. Harry had called my attention to the article as we flew to St. Thomas for a medical meeting. It is about swimming with dolphins and lists several programs, some with captive dolphins, others with wild ones. In my research I have learned of the negative effects of dolphin captivity. For that reason and my incredible experience swimming with wild dolphins at Virginia Beach, I choose one of the research groups.

The head of this group is conducting a twenty-year study with a pod of wild Atlantic Spotted Dolphins in the Bahamas. Guests on the six-day trip live on the boat, help with boat duties and assist in gathering data for the study. This program will do more than just give me an opportunity to swim with wild dolphins and live on a boat; since it is a serious research project, I can also get some reaction to my theory about the effects of dolphin sounds on humans.

Too excited to wait until I get home, I call the research office for information as soon as we reach the hotel in St. Thomas.

The brochure, along with a schedule of trips for the year, awaits me when I arrive home. Cancelling my retreat at the Monastery in Nova Scotia, I sign up for a week in May, sensing that something is about to happen that will change the direction of my life.

The information says that we will use snorkel and fins to swim with the dolphins. Diving with scuba gear seems to frighten them and this approach is more effective for closer encounters. Since I have never swum with a snorkel, I take several lessons, then practice swimming in the YMCA pool for two months preceding my departure.

In May, I excitedly board a plane from Florida to Freeport, Grand Bahama Island, where I will meet the boat. I am about to have my first encounter with the wild Atlantic Spotted Dolphins.

On the dolphin swim trip, besides me, are five other volunteer assistants, three crew members and the head of the project. The participants range in age from early twenties to a sixty-two-year-old woman who has come on eight previous trips. The research vessel is a large catamaran with billowing sails, as well as a standby motor for windless days. The boat will take us north from the West End of Grand Bahama Island to an area off the coast of Florida where the dolphins swim.

As guest research assistants, we receive detailed instructions about safety and how to live on a boat. We are told of duties each will have during the week and how to record data for the research project. Most importantly, we learn what is expected of us as we swim with the dolphins.

There is to be an attitude of respect for the dolphins and their ocean home. We are to swim with hands behind our backs, with no groping, reaching or chasing the dolphins. There are to be no more swimmers in the water than there are dolphins. We are divided into three groups of three and will alternate going in when the dolphins appear. If more dolphins appear during an encounter, more groups can go in the water. There is a serious atmosphere about the research, but there is also time for fun and games.

On the way out to dolphin territory, several hours away, we come upon several dolphins. "Dolphins on the Bow" is the signal that sends everyone forward, screaming, whistling, and beating their hands on the side of the boat.

"Does anyone want to go in?"

"I do," I say as I put on my snorkel and fins and impulsively jump in. The water is cold and rough, and I am unaccustomed to waves washing over my snorkel tube. The "Y" pool was never like this! I barely see the dolphins as they quickly swim by and soon leave. I have swallowed a quart of sea water, and immediately after I get back on board, I have that terrible green feeling creep over me.

"When you get sick," they had told us, "be sure to go to the back of the boat to throw up overboard, with the wind *behind* you."

Even though I have taken Dramamine, the excitement and sea water take their toll. I spend the next twenty-four hours below in my bunk.

By afternoon the next day, I have recovered completely, and the first thing that tastes good is salsa and chips. No gourmet meal has ever been as satisfying!

I expect the dolphins to be in a certain place, a little cove perhaps. I also think the dolphins will be around all the time. Tales from the crew and research team paint vivid pictures of glorious past encounters, personal and intimate. Here we sit, however, in the middle of the ocean, not a sign of land in sight and wait on the highest deck of the boat, gazing into the expanse of blue. Two at a time have a two-hour watch duty.

The dolphins appear only on *their* schedule. I am reminded of my vigil at Virginia Beach.

During the time spent out of the water I learn more about these dolphins for whom we wait, from books and video tapes on board, as well as informal lectures by the research head. These dolphins live in the shallow Bahama Banks where the water is about thirty feet deep and the color of a brilliant aquamarine. The Atlantic Spotted Dolphins or *Stenella frontalis* are smaller than the more familiar "Flipper"-like Bottlenose dolphins. They also seem more friendly than wild Bottlenose.

The pod with whom we will swim has interacted with humans for about twenty years. This relationship began with a salvage crew diving a sunken ship on a reef in the Bahama Banks. As the dolphins became comfortable with humans in their territorial waters, a friendship developed between them and the divers.

Interest in dolphins was reaching its height about that time with Flipper on TV and shows featuring captive dolphins. Word spread about these friendly wild dolphins and dive boats began bringing people out to swim. The same dolphins appear each year, some mothers showing off new calves. Family structure is an integral part of a pod like this, which remains together for life. Older males tend to swim together, offering protection. Mothers stay near their calves while sharing nurturing duties with aunts and other females. Teenagers or juveniles, just like their human counterparts, hang out together and are full of themselves. They race around, bumping each other in rough play like football players jostling in a locker room.

Occasionally the dolphins appear when it is my group's turn to go in. If they leave immediately, the rule still stands: when they return later the *next* group will go in. It is frustrating at times as I can only watch others in their wonderful encounters. I keep hoping my time will come.

My most frequent encounters are with the sea lice. These microscopic larvae of jellyfish choose certain people with whom they bond. The bonding results in bites that itch worse than poison ivy.

I have some trouble with my snorkel, especially when I get excited. And it is incredibly exciting when we are near the dolphins. I am fascinated that they choose to come, stay and play with us, though they have an entire ocean in which to swim. I watch as the dolphins interact with other more proficient swimmers, weaving in and out, diving and inventing games. Those who can hold their breath for long periods of time join the dolphins as they go to the bottom, pick up a sea sponge and carry it to the surface. I want so badly to have a personal encounter like the ones I am seeing and have heard about. But the dolphins seem to know those who are return swimmers and pretty much ignore me, especially since I can't do much but paddle around.

I do enjoy a sense of peace and wonder as we glide through the water with these wild creatures. It's almost like a meditation.

The most remarkable experience is that of looking into the eye of a dolphin. There is no doubt that this mammal has intelligence. When I gaze into those deep, friendly orbs, there is somebody "home" in there. And further, when they look into *my* eyes, I feel that they have touched my very soul. It is no less than a mystical experience.

My best encounter is one in which I swim alongside the researcher as she takes videos. We are completely surrounded by ten or so dolphins. I am fortunate to be a part of the pod in which they swim with their friend of many years. I find myself making a sound that comes out of the feeling I am having at the moment. It is like the sound I make when I am loving a baby, sort of an Ah-EE-Ah, but through the snorkel it becomes a squeak, not unlike some of the sounds they make. Each dolphin has a personal "signature whistle" which identifies him to other members of the pod. This becomes *my* "signature whistle."

During the week when there is free time, I discuss my dolphin-sound theory with the head of the dolphin research. I explain that I believe the communication sounds the dolphins make may have a positive effect on humans, particularly those with autism. I ask her about the possibility of doing a study. She is open to my ideas and agrees with many of them. She does warn me that to do a scientific research study on this subject would be very difficult. Even if there are positive results, it will not be easy to prove that the dolphin sounds are the reason. When the week is over, I am encouraged but cautious about the possibility of a study.

I wait all week for the private encounter I will tell everyone about when I return home. It never comes. I am confident that when I come next year, which of course I already plan to do, I will be more prepared as a swimmer. I have made a hit with the sea lice, however, and am covered with small red mementos of our time together in the water. I'll be more prepared for them too. Benadryl will be added to my list.

On the plane trip home, I try to remember details of my time in the water with the dolphins. It is so strange, but I find I can only remember the feelings, little else. All I do is sit in my seat with tears rolling down my cheeks, knowing I have had a life-changing experience. I haven't been able to journal, and now I can remember nothing. Something odd is going on, something inexplicable.

A month later, at Virginia Beach, I wake from a particularly vivid and wonderful dream. As I lie there, I don't want to move for fear of erasing the feeling the dream has left with me. As soon as I become completely awake, it is gone — both the memory and the feeling. I realize this is similar to what happens with the dolphin experience. As soon as the conscious mind clicks in, the awesome experience in the water seems to disappear.

I go down for my walk on the beach and write the lyrics to my first song.

The Bliss

From dream awaking,
A feeling lingers.
You try to hold it,
It slips through your fingers.
Woe and Wonder intermingle.
It's like the dream,
Even better,
Like.....

High on the bridge the watch we're keeping,
Eyes and ears attuned to blue.
Waiting for signs of agile leaping,
Ever ancient, ever new.

Is that a fin or just a shadow?
Is that a whistle or just the winds?
Anticipation, like some lover
Waits for one whom destiny sends.

Suddenly here, they're all around us,
Streaking through water, playing the bow.
Choosing to stay and share their beauty,
Sharing their joy of here and now.

Then for a time we swim together.
Dreaming, I've imagined this.
Soon they are gone, the magic ended.
All I remember is The Bliss.

From dream awaking,
A feeling lingers.
You try to hold it,
It slips through your fingers.
Woe and wonder intermingle.
It's like the dream,
Even better,
Like LOVE.

All I remember is The Bliss.

Libby Layne will eventually learn that what she experienced in the water with the dolphins is almost always true. Others who have swum with them agree. It's as if while swimming with the dolphins, time becomes as it is here: there is no past or future, only the wonder of the present moment. Do you begin to notice that much of what you experience on earth is just like eternity? Think about it!

June 1992

I return for another week with the research group. The boat is different, the guests are different, the dolphins are the same but even better. My swimming and snorkeling skills have improved significantly this year, resulting in longer and more exciting encounters. My encounters with the sea lice have also significantly improved — for them! It seems once they have had a taste of you and like you, they single you out even more the next year.

I continue to use my "signature sound," hoping someday they will recognize it. I still wait for that "special encounter" that eludes me.

The final night I share my song "The Bliss," which I composed after last year's trip, with those on board. They all agree I have captured the essence of the dolphin encounter experience.

I have decided to conduct my own study, observing children with autism as they are exposed to the dolphin sounds. I discuss my tentative plans with the research head who, though she will not be involved, is agreeable to answering questions which might arise. I will need input such as this to ensure that my study is as scientific as is possible. From recordings of the dolphin communications used in her research, a commercial tape and CD have been made and are available to the public. I receive her permission to use them.

I feel confident and excited about my study. I am grateful that the research head will be there to advise me when I need it. It is all coming together!

I am excited too! I enjoy seeing Libby Layne so confident that after all the years of working her life puzzle, she sees a picture finally taking shape. The picture that is appearing is quite unusual and mysterious. Will she be able to make sense of it?

September, 1992

After my second swim trip in June with the research dolphin group, I return home anxious to make definite plans for my study .

The first step is to pull together the information I have gathered for twenty-five years. To give credibility to my study, I ask the head of the Arts Department at Radford University to meet and advise me on procedure. He suggests that I write a summary of all my research leading up to my conclusion that dolphin sounds might have a positive effect on the autistic person. After reviewing this, he will offer some suggestions as to what I might do next.

In the twenty-five years since I first was introduced to dolphins, I have collected articles, books, audio and video tapes, and files full of notes from conferences and my own experiences. I sort through volumes of information on dolphins, autism, and sound therapy, astounded at the amount and depth of my research. What had begun as a mere interest, a fascinating pastime, has grown into a body of research that might well be of some importance. As I write my summary, confidence in my theory grows.

It is important to me that my study show what is *actually* happening when the dolphin sounds are tested, not just what I *want* to happen. I realize this will be difficult, since my scientific experience is almost nonexistent. I could never even memorize scientific method in high school.

In addition to my dolphin expert, the research head, I need someone with expertise in sound therapy. I learn of a man in North Carolina who is studying the effects of sound frequencies on the brain. I contact him, go to North Carolina, and share my theory and hopes of doing a study. He is very interested. This dovetails quite well with some of his research. He agrees to help in evaluating my results with state-of-the-art sound equipment used in his work.

He also advises me on the use of EEG tests to determine the effects of the dolphin sounds on brain wave patterns.

He is so interested in my plans that he asks me to write an article for his newsletter. This newsletter features new research in sound therapies and the brain and would be sent all over the world. I contact the publisher and begin writing the article. I quickly realize it is much too soon for this. I just don't have enough information. I send a letter to the publisher explaining that I'll do the article at a later date.

In January, the newsletter arrives in the mail, and as I look through it, a headline leaps off the page, "Link Between Autism and Dolphin Sounds Studied."

I am surprised, of course, having decided to write the article later. I am almost afraid to read it; if I hadn't written it, who had? I had shared very little with the man in North Carolina and had sent no written material. What could he have possibly put together from what I had told him? I begin reading the article and my heart stops. In the first paragraph is the statement that the dolphin research group, with whom I had gone swimming, was "working with people with autism." This is completely untrue; their work is exclusively with the dolphins. Knowing how very protective the researcher is about her work and her reputation, I expect the worst.

I place a call to the research head immediately, explaining the situation, as well as faxing a copy of the article and the letter I had sent to the publisher. Thank goodness I had kept it! I had not written the article, I explain, nor had I given permission for anything to be written. I ask if there is anything I can do to rectify the situation? She is absolutely furious and lets me know in no uncertain terms that she is greatly disappointed in me.

I call the sound researcher, who admits to writing the article. He is very apologetic and agrees to print a retraction immediately. He will also place a personal call to the dolphin research head to apologize and exonerate me.

But the damage has been done. Wanting nothing more to do with me or my study, the dolphin researcher withdraws any further help. She does suggest that I might call Dr. Betsy Smith in Florida and gives me her phone number.

I can't believe it! Things had been going so smoothly, one step after the other, everything falling into place. I can't understand why this has happened, and though I always look at the positive, I can't find one good thing about this! How could this be a piece of the puzzle? It seems more likely some cat had jumped up on the table, knocked it over and scattered the pieces all over the floor!

It is time to take my ritual sorting-out, prayer walk. I remind myself of two long-held beliefs: the first, that we can choose to be thankful or "Praise God in all things"; the second, that no matter what the situation, the positive will eventually outweigh the negative. At this moment, I am not at all sure I believe either one. Though I find this situation a difficult one for which to be thankful, I force myself to do it anyway. With very little enthusiasm I say, "Thank you for what has just happened."

I know she is disappointed, and I can feel her frustration. But she is doing the right thing. Something shifts when a human being chooses to be thankful for whatever happens and lets go of certain expectations. It allows space for other possibilities God may have in mind. If that space is already filled, a real opportunity may be missed. How often we here see human beings getting in the way of the very thing they want most.

Home from her walk, she feels more hopeful and, after getting up her nerve, calls Dr. Betsy Smith in Florida.

She picks up puzzle pieces, rearranges them, and finds a piece that was there all the time; she just hadn't tried it. The new piece will fill in a big space and will move her closer to solving the mystery of the Sound of the Dolphin's Psalm.

As I dial Dr. Betsy Smith's number, I am nervous. This woman has been a hero of mine for many years. Who was I to just call her out of the blue? Would she think I was presumptuous?

I needn't have worried. The "famous Dr. Betsy Smith" turns out to be just "Betsy" and soon we are chatting as though we had known each other for years.

After giving a summary of the research and experiences leading up to my theory, I suggest the possibility that dolphin communication sounds may have been a factor in her study. In that study, almost twenty years earlier, many positive changes had been observed in autistic children swimming with captive dolphins. To my surprise, Betsy confesses she had suspected this might be true but had never followed up on the idea. When she learns Harry and I will vacation in Florida at the end of February, she immediately invites us to her home.

"We can talk about your study, and perhaps I can help you set it up," Betsy offers.

I am beside myself. Even *I* couldn't have dreamed up a better scenario! Someone seems to know more about this than I do and is keeping one step ahead of me.

As we drive through Florida the next month, we see the path taken by Hurricane Andrew as it roared through the area a year before. The destruction can still be seen everywhere; it looks as if a bomb has exploded. There are hundreds of abandoned houses and businesses. Huge trees have been pulled up by their roots and thrown aside like Tinker Toys. Rebuilding will take a long time.

In a small town that suffered great losses during the storm, we find Betsy's house, still standing and with little damage. We park the RV in the driveway where we will spend the night. A little "star-struck," I meet Betsy, her husband and teenage son — friendly, down-to-earth people. Why is it so surprising when we find that famous people are just *people* after all? Betsy goes into the kitchen and fixes a wonderful chicken dinner which we enjoy with the family.

Betsy and I talk, nonstop, until late that night. She discusses details of the study she conducted years before and gives me some practical suggestions for the study I am planning. She says it would not be difficult to set up a semi-scientific study to test the dolphin/sound hypothesis. Best of all, she offers to be an advisor to help me in any way she can. This is more than I had ever expected, and I am excited and encouraged once again.

Betsy also tells me of her new venture called SEA (Society for Environmental Awareness). This membership organization's goal is to improve the environment of sea mammals, particularly dolphins. Realizing that the captivity of dolphins is something she can no longer support, Betsy has discontinued her work at a captive dolphin facility in Florida. Her dream is to build a center where she can work with children and *wild* dolphins. Others could come to be with the dolphins as well as to do research. The Society, Betsy says, might even be able to help fund my study. She gives me the phone number of a couple in Texas who are heading up the project and suggests I call them.

There is one more problem. I have no swim program for my annual dolphin swim. I feel it would be awkward to return to the research vessel and that I would not be particularly welcome. I want so much to go again and ask Betsy if she knows of anyone else who has swim programs.

"Horace Dobbs asked me to go on a trip to the Bahamas in July this year with Rebecca Fitzgerald and Dolphinswim. I can't go, why don't you go in my place?"

"Go in your place? But they want Dr. Betsy Smith, famous researcher, not Miss Nobody from Virginia."

"Don't worry, I'll just tell him we are working together and you are my representative." This was better than I could have ever imagined!

Libby Layne sort of puffs up like a proud peacock, feeling a little more "cocky" than is good for her. But time will take care of that, and another valuable lesson will be learned.

Dolphinswim, July, 1993

This trip is completely different from the dolphin research swim trip. The overall purpose of this experience is swimming with the dolphins, enjoying the encounters, and sharing with other members of the group. The boat is larger, and instead of six guests, there are fifteen. Instead of only the United States being represented, there are participants from all over the world. And this is no "ship of fools"; the intellectual level is quite high, and conversations are stimulating and challenging.

When I meet Rebecca, the head of Dolphinswim, I am immediately drawn to her. Amazingly, her eyes are exactly like those of a dolphin. As we make eye contact, it is like meeting an old friend, though it is our first encounter. She is beautiful both inside and out, a perfect hostess for all her guests, sharing her joy and enthusiasm with everyone.

I have two cabin mates, Kris from Brussels, Belgium, and Noel from the Netherlands. Other guests are from Germany, Switzerland, England, Canada, Japan and the USA.

Dr. Horace Dobbs, the English author who has written many books about dolphins, is the "facilitator" on this trip. He will share his expertise with guests in evening sessions. With him is a Japanese man named Dr. Masato Nakagawa. Dr. Nakagawa has brought with him a large following of Japanese. My favorite of these is Shizuko, the interpreter. She is a tiny, vivacious woman who speaks four languages. There is a delightful, posh, Englishwoman who has taken the name Delphine Starr for her work involving dolphins. It is a varied and congenial group, and the dolphins are gracious and give us some beautiful encounters.

As my swimming and snorkeling skills improve, so do my encounters with the dolphins. I love being able to go in every time the dolphins arrive — no waiting in groups or worrying that I will do the wrong thing at the wrong time. There is still an atmosphere of profound respect for the dolphins. As Rebecca makes clear, we are guests in their world; we must be *courteous* guests. One disadvantage to everyone going in at once is that when there are only two dolphins, they are easily frightened away when fifteen swimmers splash into the water.

Early one morning, before any of the other guests are up and about, I spot four or five dolphins right next to the boat. A crew member gives me permission to go in. Since I will be swimming alone, he will watch me from the deck. I am so excited at the prospect of having an encounter between only the dolphins and me, that I too-hurriedly put on my gear. As I enter the water, my mask immediately begins leaking. I am miserable; I have four dolphins all to myself, they are ready to play, and I can't do a thing. I reluctantly return to the boat to readjust my mask strap, fearing the dolphins will leave and I'll have missed my chance. The dolphins remain, however, and as other swimmers join the encounter, we swim for over an hour. I have had no breakfast and finally become exhausted. Though the dolphins stay, I realize it is time for me to get out, and as the little Zodiak pickup boat stops near me, I get aboard.

Exhilarated from my encounter and my beautiful surroundings, I spontaneously begin singing "Oh What a Beautiful Morning." Shizuko, the little Japanese interpreter is also in the Zodiak and says, "That's my favorite American song," and together we raise our voices in a common expression of the joy of the moment.

My "near-miss" encounter taught me to always take my time in preparing to enter the water. In my zeal to get in before anyone else, I had wasted precious time and risked missing the whole experience. From now on I will relax a little more in the knowledge that if the dolphins want to play, they will stay around.

Dr. Nakagawa, Horace's guest, is considered a healer, using what the Japanese call Ki energy, or in Chinese, Chi. This energy, they believe, is the life force that causes people to be healthy; blockage or misuse of this Ki energy causes illness. Dr. Dobbs is exploring the possibility that dolphins may also have this energy. He wonders if this might be a factor in what he has observed when people with depression seem to be healed when they swim with the dolphins.

There will be experiments using this Ki energy with people on board. It is not required that anyone attend the sessions or believe any of the energy theories. I am not really sure about all of this "woo, woo" as I call it. I find it particularly suspect when one of the Japanese begins "channelling" the dolphins, who are telling her what they are thinking and when they'll show up. She only speaks Japanese, so I suppose the dolphins are multilingual. I keep an open mind, however, and enjoy hearing both the new information and becoming aware of my own limits in what I will accept as truth. I am comfortable simply enjoying the dolphins and the international flavor of the trip.

We have another "dolphin day" during which they come, eight or nine of them, off-and-on for two or three hours. Because I am more proficient in diving down into the water with my snorkel now, I am able to have some wonderful personal encounters. For no particular reason, I dive as deeply as I am able. As I turn and begin swimming toward the surface, there is a tiny, grey baby dolphin plastered to the front of my body. He remains there as we rise through the clear blue water, simultaneously breaking into the sunlight in a burst of joyous companionship. I only wish I were able to leap four feet out of the water as he did. I certainly felt like it!

During the week I become quite friendly with Dr. Dobbs, or Horace, as he wishes to be called. He asks me to read the children's book he is writing and offer suggestions, which I am just "cheeky" enough to do. He is pleased with my comments and takes some of my constructive criticisms. Near the end of the week he asks me if I would help him get his book published in America. I am feeling quite encouraged about the way things are going. I am becoming a member of the dolphin "in-crowd." Not only do I know Betsy Smith who wants to become involved in my study, I am helping Horace Dobbs in his worldwide organization to promote the betterment of their environment. This is getting exciting!

Libby Layne is really feeling very important now. This is what you humans call an "ego trip," and she is enjoying the ride. It won't hurt to let her get "puffed up" for just a little while. If it gets out of hand, we may have to burst her bubble.

The last day of the trip Horace asks for my address to keep in touch about his book. When I write my name as "Elizabeth W. Jarrett," Horace asks, "What is this Elizabeth foolishness? I thought your name was Libby."

Without a second thought I reply, "Actually, my name is Libby Layne."

"That's it, it's perfect," he laughs, "It's what you do in the water with the dolphins." With his hand he makes a dolphin-like motion chanting, "Libby Layne, Libby Layne, Libby Layne."

This seems to be a subtle hint not to take myself so seriously, not to get too grown-up. In my frolicking with the dolphins I am taken back to that childlike place of wonder and enchantment. The experience with the baby dolphin had been as near heaven as anything I had experienced on earth.

"Lest ye become as a little child,
ye shall not enter the kingdom of heaven."

It is so nice to have Libby Layne back to Libby Layne again. From this day on, she will use her little girl name for any work she does for and with dolphins. The baby dolphin had helped her remember the place inside where her playful self, her little girl self, still lived. How wonderful it was for me to be a part of her "heavenly" experience.

There are many heavenly experiences to be found right on earth, you know. Humans too often forget this and are living their lives waiting only for a heaven somewhere in the future. After all, didn't Jesus say that the Kingdom of God was within?

Before I return to Virginia, I spend a few days in Miami. Here I again meet with Betsy Smith. We are joined by the development people from Texas and others who are also interested in SEA (Betsy's new venture) and the center Betsy wants to build. They are considering different places around the world where it might be located.

The Development Director, Arlene, and I immediately become friends, and before the weekend is over, I have accepted the title, Associate Development Director, meaning I agree to invest some money and help get the project started. The developers have impressive materials about one site for the center, which I will take home for review by a business manager. For years I had been looking for that *special* project into which I could invest my heart, my time and my resources. At the center, I could do my study with Betsy to oversee it. I feel confident that all the years of learning about dolphins, autism and sound therapy were leading to this moment. This puts together all the puzzle pieces. I now have the whole picture.

Arlene asks me to write an article for the SEA Newsletter which will launch the campaign to make the Society for Environmental Awareness a worldwide organization. I have hit the "Big Time." I am on the brink of something wonderful! This is IT!

WRONG! A year later, the SEA Board of directors has realized the time is not right for building a center. "Don't send any money," says Betsy.

"We only signed up a few members," says Arlene.

The whole plan fizzles to nothing but wishful thinking.

Throwing my fancy business cards with "Libby Layne, Associate Development Director" printed on them in the trash, I again wonder, "Where do I go from here?"

It seems we didn't have to burst her bubble after all. The natural process of life did it on its own.

When the SEA venture falls through, it appears once again that Libby Layne has lost a piece of her puzzle. She was positive this one was a sure fit and is disappointed. Yet, this lesson is a familiar one she has met several times before on her journey with the dolphins; when the piece doesn't fit, start looking for another.

IX
Fantasia

February, 1994

Lent has become a special time for me in recent years. In the Church of the Brethren, where I went as a child, not only was Lent not observed, the word was never used. Not until my college days did I attend an Episcopal Church and discover a form of worship I would grow to love. Though it was entirely different from my early years, I felt strangely at home with the chants, liturgies, and praying from *The Book of Common Prayer* as I knelt on the prayer benches. The observance of each season of the Church year, particularly the forty days of Lent, gave Easter a whole new meaning for me.

Each year at the onset of Lent, I attend the Ash Wednesday service at my church. During my prayers I ask to be assigned a discipline to do or not to do, to work on or work through. Sometimes it's just a little thing, sometimes it's more complicated. There are times I don't do anything at all and just listen for awhile — which I find to be the most difficult!

This year my message is very clear: *"Get your dolphin room ready for your study!"*

After leaving the school we started, my friend Patricia became a licensed counselor. She set up her practice in a little house and created what she called a "sacred space." It is similar to what we had dreamed the school would be. Many children come to this special place and receive help in unique ways. Some do art or sand play, some tell stories. She does regular counseling but knows there is a spiritual component to helping people heal. We have stayed in contact but have not worked together for several years.

"Do you have any room in your building I could use for my study?" I ask.

"People are always asking about the room upstairs but nothing has felt right. This sounds perfect," she answers.

We work out a plan: I will be responsible for fixing up the room and can then use it for a small fee. We are both excited about sharing the same space and having a common goal again. It appears the dream we shared might come true yet. We will be helping troubled children and adults in new and exciting ways.

I need a special name for my study so I head out for my meditation and prayer walk in hopes of an inspiration. It isn't long before I imagine the word *DOLFA* with an *F* not a *PH*. Thinking it must be an anagram, that each of these letters must stand for one word, I try to figure out what they might be. The *D* is for *Dolphin*, of course, the *FA*, *For Autism*, but what is the *OL* in the middle? How about *offers language, overtone language, optimum learning*?

None of them had the right sound or feeling.

I am very pleased. She is opening up more and more to what is available to her here. She received the message very well and at least has the name of her study correct, though there is more to it than she knows. This is an example of a situation in which we give some of the information but not all. You see, if Libby Layne had known everything about DOLFA at the beginning, she may not have learned all her lessons along the way. I have discovered that she sometimes plunges headlong into something, believing she has it all figured out. I thought this best; she'll know what it means at the right time.

She adds the word WAVE to DOLFA since she will be working with sound waves. She wonders if the sounds the dolphins make are a special vibration when they reach the human brain. There are Alpha-Waves and Beta Waves; this could be called a "DOLFA-WAVE." She's getting close!

During the forty days of Lent, I prepare my Dolphin Room. Using videos from my own dolphin swims as a model, I create a room that appears to be underwater. Although the children aren't actually swimming with the dolphins, the room where they listen to the sounds will be as much like the ocean as possible.

Everything in the room is decorated in shades of aquamarine blue, simulating the waters of the Bahama Banks. The walls are painted a light aqua, the trim, a darker shade. The window blinds are yet another hue, and soft, multicolored pastel silk scarfs, swaying like sea plants, hang as curtains at two windows. The plush carpet is mottled and has the look of the white sand on the ocean floor which reflects the blue of the water. On the ceiling, an artist has used a sponge to paint over the rough spackle in varying shades of white, blue and yellow. Radiating from the light fixture are yellow circles, creating the illusion that you are underwater with sunshine coming through. There are two large mirrors in one corner, reflecting the blue of the walls. There is no furniture, and the only objects in the room will be the sound equipment. As I choose everything for the room, I feel I am being guided every step of the way. People who enter the room say it feels magical, safe, even "womb-like." This is just what I have in mind. It is important that autistic children feel safe.

I love Libby Layne's Dolphin Room. It makes me feel at home — "my heavenly home," I mean. Many humans throughout history have tried to explain what eternity is like. Artists have painted with wonderful colors, musicians have composed celestial music and writers have written stories and poetry telling of the wonders of this state of being called heaven or eternity. Some of them are at least partly right. Yet none of them can completely describe the way it really is. It is one of those things you have to experience yourself. Just like the way time is different here, so are colors, sounds and feelings. Even being here, there are really no words I could use to fully explain the wonder of it. You'll just have to wait, I guess.

When I had talked with the man in North Carolina about my study, he encouraged me to get state-of-the-art sound equipment to keep the dolphin sounds as pure as possible with no interference. With help from a sound technician, I choose an excellent CD player, an amplifier, a tape player, and two speakers. When I finish my selecting, I notice a piece of equipment called an equalizer. It has all sorts of levers and lights and looks very complicated. For some reason, I keep going back to it. I finally ask, "What does this do?"

"It tunes in and out various sound frequencies. You can adjust each band of sound from highest to lowest."

"I don't know why, but I think I need this too." I have simply stopped questioning these strong leadings and just "do it." I ask the man who has sold me all of this expensive equipment to install it in the room and leave, quite pleased with myself.

I make a call to Betsy Smith who suggests ways of keeping the study as scientific as possible. Betsy and two other professionals — a pediatrician specializing in children with learning problems and a woman who does AIT (Audio- Integration-Therapy) — will be my advisors during the study and review any results I may have afterwards.

Making it official, I have DOLFA-1 put on my license plate and open a DOLFA-WAVE bank account. My daughter Amy, an artist, designs a logo that represents what I am doing. The dolphin in the logo is shaded with sound wave patterns as they would be seen on a audiogram. I order stationery bearing the logo and a business card with all my names. It reads:

DOLFA-WAVE
"Libby Layne"
Elizabeth Wampler Jarrett MEd

I am hoping this time I won't have to throw them away!

My next task is to plan exactly how I will conduct the sessions. Experience in previous sessions for AIT had found twenty minutes to be a satisfactory time frame. I decide to use this as the length of time each child will be in the dolphin room while the dolphin sounds play over the sound system. During this time, I will play with, talk to, or do whatever seems appropriate for each particular child. Basically, each session will be tailor-made to the individual.

I will video tape each of eight sessions, two each week for a month, which will be reviewed by my three advisors. Parents will also be given forms for recording changes in behaviors at home. I know that there are too many variables, making my study less than scientific, but I accept this and hope for the best.

There is one more very important question: who are the subjects for my study? Where are the children and how will I find them?

"They'll appear," I say confidently. "I wouldn't have been guided this far if the children weren't going to come."

With that statement, I place my complete faith in a Plan that is not my own and the guidance which comes from the Source of that Plan.

How thrilled I am to hear this statement coming from Libby Layne! This understanding will influence everything she does from now on. She is listening and waiting, two things that are extremely important, but very difficult for her. It is her faith, above all, that will assure the Plan's success.

So where are those children? Libby Layne is trying to be patient. I know that they are out there waiting for her. What brings them to her is a situation arranged years before when she was also waiting and listening.

It seems logical to seek an organization which has access to parents of children with autism. It suddenly occurs to me that I had been involved with just such an organization when I did my practicum. The Arc, which it is now called, might be willing to publish a small article in their newsletter telling of my study and asking for volunteers.

I write a short description of my study and mail it to The Arc office. The newsletter will come out in August, giving me plenty of time for beginning my study the first of October. Within a week of sending the description to The Arc, my phone begins to ring. Parents are asking if their child might be part of the study. How, I ask them, do they know about it?

"We received a letter from The Arc office," they reply.

I am pleased, grateful and feel an enormous trust shown me by The Arc's actions. They are very protective of families of the children with disabilities. Thanks to them, I receive calls from enough parents to choose four participants for my study.

I am in awe of the way pieces of the past fit into this wonderful puzzle, even as I work it in the present.

Good observation, Libby Layne! You have experienced an example of how the Plan for a person's life can be such a mystery. Situations from the past, appearing to have no importance at the time, can be key connections in the present.

This only applies to humans, of course. Here we see the whole Plan at once.

It is likely that because The Arc has seen her working well with families in setting up Parent to Parent, they trust that she won't be involved with something that will hurt anyone, even though this is something new and different.

Parents of the four autistic children are sent forms to be filled out, telling Libby Layne all about these precious gifts who have been sent for her study. Before she begins working in the Dolphin Room, she will go to each of the children's homes to meet them.

Everything is in place.

X
Rhapsody

September, 1994

The four participants for my study had been chosen somehow by the forces which had been guiding my life to this juncture. Each was a unique individual with a personality that shone through even the deepest levels of this debilitating disorder, a disorder which mystifies the experts and creates in its wake parents who become passionate advocates for new and innovative treatments. Perhaps the next treatment will bring their child back to them.

These parents are the heroes who refuse to believe their children's condition is irreversible. They believe in miracles, spend endless hours and countless dollars, and never give up. I was being allowed by a group of these heroes to take their children into a world of dolphin sounds. Would this be the miracle for which they waited? "Why," they would ask, "are you so interested in autistic children? Did someone in your family have it or some other disability?" How many times I have been asked this through the years — through the years with Pringle, Very Special Arts, and ARC, the years of reading everything I could find about autism and other brain dysfunctions. I have always answered, "I have no idea," knowing only of my passion to enrich these children's lives and to help comfort their parents' grief and pain. There must be a connection somewhere, but it is a mystery.

Anxiously, I await the moment when I will finally meet the children of DOLFA-WAVE.

The first is Dylan...

A bizarre world is enclosed in this room, one I recognize immediately as the world of imitation used in the TV movie *Son Rise*. The movie, and later the book, had fifteen years ago sparked my interest in the disorder called autism. The young boy in the movie had been brought out of his autism by a method developed by his parents using love, acceptance and entry into his strange, repetitive behaviors. These parents subsequently developed a center in Massachusetts where they teach their techniques to other parents of autistic children. It was to this center that Dylan and his mother went for a month, participating in the program there. Afterwards, Dylan's mother trained volunteers here at their home in the techniques she learned at the center. Sessions had continued in this room at his home for the two years since that time.

I watch through the two-way mirror on the door as his mother sits, tapping on the floor, a response to the same tapping from Dylan a moment before. The room is stark white; no distractions. Only two toy shelves placed far above eye level break the monotony of the room in which the two sit. His mother introduces a large rubber ball. Without looking at her, he takes the ball, places it on the floor in front of him and begins spinning it with both hands, eyes transfixed.

His mother repeats the behavior with another ball saying, "See the ball — do you want the ball?"

She puts brightly colored stickers on her forehead, encouraging him to look at her, to make eye contact. Constantly she imitates, encourages and touches Dylan, accepting his repetitive behaviors, his distant stare.

It is eerie watching this scene. I had been captivated as I watched the TV movie and hoped someday to use this method with an autistic child. Though I had tried some of the mimicking techniques with Pringle, he was not really autistic. Dylan is the first child "diagnosed" with autism I have ever observed. He and his mother sit, facing each other, doing precisely what I had seen in the movie. The providence of it all brings tears to my eyes.

I gaze at this beautiful five-year-old little boy exhibiting behaviors associated with this mysterious disorder. He makes little or no eye contact and stares vacantly into space. Occasionally he smiles faintly at something his mother does. It is a fleeting gesture but lights up the room. Any toy introduced is quickly placed on the floor in front of him. With one hand or the other, he spins it around and around, fixing his eyes on the object. He never initiates a touch or hug, but accepts these from his mother. He allows but does not participate. When he has had enough attention, he begins walking around the room on his tiptoes. He is tall for his age, and this clumsy posture causes him to fall frequently. Rhythmically with his hand he strikes the floor, "tap, tap, tap" as his mother answers, "tap, tap, tap," mimicking his every move.

Each one of these repetitive behaviors is called a "self-stimulatory" behavior (self-stim) or "ism." They are found in all autistic individuals and range from mild to severe. The behaviors vary in kind but the patterns are similar and the results are the same — a withdrawal from the sensory world as we know it. The child partially or completely removes himself from everyone, including parents and family, into a world of his own. The pain of this withdrawal is especially acute when, as in Dylan's case, a child is born perfectly normal and develops into a vivacious, communicative child, then becomes autistic.

I had read in his history form that at the age of one year Dylan began having seizures. Soon thereafter his autistic behaviors manifested, with Dylan losing his fifteen to twenty word vocabulary and completely withdrawing from his family. His seizures continued, not responding to traditional anti-convulsive drug treatment. He had recently been on a special diet for seizure control, administered by Johns Hopkins Hospital, called the Katogenic Diet. This seemed to reduce the frequency of his seizures which had been occurring every few minutes during the day and night. Throughout Dylan's short life, his parents have sought answers and treatments with only minimal success in AIT (Audio-Integration-Therapy) and the method now being used in this small room. The child of that first year has been lost to them.

Dylan appears to be soothed by soft rhythmic singing and will occasionally vocalize when the singing stops. Very fast or loud rhythms tend to increase his self-stim. He may respond to a little squeak in the floor but will ignore a loud noise. He is probably more hearing deficient (hypoacute) than having overactive hearing (hyperacute). It is difficult to determine what autistic children can hear and what they just ignore. It was noted at one diagnostic session that when he was turning objects or tapping, his EEG showed his brain completely relaxed. His parents have used several sound therapy tapes, and he has gone through Audio-Integration-Training (AIT) twice, with some improvement regarding increased awareness and responsiveness to sound. Water has a calming effect on Dylan, but his mother associates this more with feeling than sound. There was a time, his mother said, when the bath water "trickled" after being turned off, which caused Dylan to giggle, not a regular response from him unless physically tickled.

After watching at the window for a time, his mother allows me to enter the room. He acknowledges my presence with a glance, then goes back to spinning his ball. I imitate his tapping and turning, following his mother's lead. He allows me in the play but shows no interest in my being there. His mother leaves the room, and I am left alone with Dylan. I am somewhat uneasy in this new, yet familiar setting. As I relax and follow my instincts, being with him seems perfectly natural. He is detached but allows me to continue with activities his mother had begun. I reach out slowly, playing the "nose game" I had used with Pringle. At first he draws away, then lets me touch his nose.

I begin singing *Oom-Pa-Pa*, a rhythmic song Pringle had liked. As I sing, he vocalizes with me and continues after I stop as if signaling me to begin again. He seems comfortable in my presence, and I am pleased to be accepted into his world.

His mother watches through the two-way mirror and is encouraged at Dylan's response to me. She is, as most parents of children with autism, open to any possibility that might help. The next session will be in the Dolphin Room in October.

Then there is Kim...

Completely ignoring me, Kim gets out of her mother's car and walks into her house. I have arrived early and am waiting in their driveway.

Kim is to be the only female and the only adult in my study. She is 28 years old but looks much younger. Oblivious to my presence, she gets a drink from the fridge, and then begins opening and shutting cabinet doors again and again. As her mother and I talk, she is in constant motion, wandering in and out of the room, flipping lights off and on, turning on and off the TV. These are Kim's unique self-stim behaviors — different, yet the same repetitive, rhythmic patterns that characterize autistic behavior.

Kim was virtually nonverbal until the age of six and would only scream and cry for attention. Her mother was positive something was very wrong, but at that time little was known about autism and other neurological disorders. She experienced what so many parents of that era faced — a frustrating search for any clues to her child's problems and a medical world which offered no hope.

At the age of six, Kim began having Grand Mal seizures. She became a behavioral problem with self-abuse tendencies and was constantly agitated.

From the ages of six to eight, she attended a residential program at the Dejarnette Center for Human Development. Her mother believes it "saved her life." Through a behavioral modification program, Kim became a calm, docile and pleasant child. This behavior has continued until the present. At the Dejarnette, she also developed language skills, increasing her vocabulary and using two and three word sentences. She was cooperative and related well to her peers. She was even heard to sing the first few bars of *Jesus Loves Me*. Though her mother wanted her to remain there another year, the staff felt they had done all they could do. Back at home, she was enrolled in a Special Education program in the county public schools.

Her seizures ceased when she was twelve years old. Her language skills suddenly returned to nonverbal, a change which her mother relates to some unknown trauma. Kim has recently responded positively to Facilitated Communication (FC). This is a method used with nonverbal individuals using a spelling card or computer keyboard. The trained professional gently holds the client's hand, allowing them to type out messages. Though this technique is highly controversial, Kim's mother is convinced that Kim is one who, indeed, was able to show her intelligence through this method. From reading transcripts of the FC, Kim's mother believes she is intelligent, has dreams, remembers her past and has very deep feelings and beliefs. During the past three or four months, Kim has refused to communicate in this way. She has indicated through her Facilitated Communication that she *can* talk but does not wish to do so. In her FC, Kim indicated a reason for this refusal; someone said she sounded retarded.

Kim enjoys music. She remains quiet and calm when she hears low pitches but becomes quite anxious, clasps her hands and walks around or rocks back and forth on her legs when there are loud or high pitches. In a setting away from home, loud music and noises excite her to the point where she has to leave. When her hearing was tested at an AIT facility, it was determined to be hyperacute, perhaps three times the norm. When she is enjoying music, she rocks, claps her hands and smiles. The sound of ocean surf is very disturbing and frightens her greatly. I wonder whether the water sounds on the dolphin CDs will bother her.

Taking her mother's lead, I talk openly, assuming that Kim understands every word. As we talk, she occasionally wanders through the room. I ask her permission to inquire about her history. She makes eye contact with me, attends to my question, but makes no response. Her mother suggests that Kim use her communication board to answer; she refuses. We tell her that we will continue unless she lets us know otherwise.

My attempt at getting her attention, using one of my "kid" songs, backfires as she becomes very irritated. Her mother suggests I may have insulted her, treating her like a child. I try another approach. On a completely adult level, I explain what the DOLFA-WAVE study is and what we will be doing together. I tell her about swimming with dolphins, explaining that they communicate, but like her, they don't speak. I request her help with the study, as she is the only adult participating. Perhaps, I suggest, she could communicate her experience with her mother by FC. This conversation lasts for at least five minutes, during which Kim's eye contact with me is constant and intense. She never takes her eyes off mine and appears to be taking in every word. I assume eye contact is not an issue with Kim. When I speak to her mother as I leave, she tells me that what Kim has just done with me she has never seen her do with anyone except herself. The intensity of Kim's attention is extremely rare. I am pleased and encouraged that Kim will be a welcome addition to my study.

Then comes James...

Like a tornado, five-year-old James whirls around the room, ignoring the fact that there is a stranger in his house. With dark hair and mischievous eyes, he immediately captivates me. He never stops; even when he watches TV he jumps on a little trampoline strategically placed in front of it. His vocabulary is limited, but he communicates constantly with his mother and his older sister. He is quite rough with both of them, running around, hitting and jumping. Though he ignores me, he finds ways of disrupting conversation and diverting his mother's attention. She is firm but allows him his space.

James, like Dylan, had a normal birth and developed normally until he was twelve months old. At this time he had language skills, made eye contact and was not hyperactive. By the time he was eighteen months old, he had totally withdrawn. He stopped talking and had up to one hundred tantrums a day. He was diagnosed with Pervasive Development Disorder with hyperactivity and possibly an Attention Deficit. Though he was not diagnosed autistic, he has many autistic behaviors. The withdrawal, loss of language, limited eye-contact, and hyperacute hearing are all present. His mother discovered his acute hearing when he woke up screaming every night at a specific time. She finally became aware that a train whistle was blowing in the distance at the exact time of James's awakenings. When he was tested, it was confirmed that his hearing was extremely sensitive, even painful. He participated in AIT sessions twice, with impressive results each time. His language skills increased, especially in comprehension. He became more social. He is on the Feingold diet to control his hyperactivity and at one time was on Ritalin. The Ritalin caused mood rebounding and has been discontinued. He still has a problem with aggressive behavior, and his social relating is in the form of rough horseplay. He is very affectionate with those he trusts and welcomes being touched and hugged.

Sound is an important component in James's life, both in a positive and negative way. He loves music sung by children and classical music such as *The Nutcracker* and *Fantasia*. He enjoys playing his mother's guitar and dances to music he likes. Music must not be too loud or in the high frequency levels. Sounds of trains, fans, blowing wind, and malls or restaurants where there are many people and echoes bother him.

James's mother is very knowledgeable about his disorder and has worked with other children like him. Very involved in his life, she is a typical activist parent, seeking new information and any idea that might help her child.

The entire time I am there in discussion with his mother, James ignores me. It is as if I don't exist in his world, which, in fact, I don't. He acknowledges only those he trusts and guards his space jealously. This one will be a challenge!

Finally, with Patrick...

Again, I am being ignored! This time it's by an eleven-year-old, sitting quietly on the sofa, absorbed in a TV program. Handsome and well-built, Patrick looks at me only when his mother says, "Say hello to Libby, Patrick."

"Hello Libby, Libby," he says, immediately returning to his program.

As he watches, I hear him repeating, verbatim, phrases and words from the characters on TV. This is another common autistic behavior: ecolalia, or mimicking without any particular meaning or comprehension of another's words. Behaviors of this kind are repetitive, ritualistic, and become a constant companion of those who are autistic. It keeps their world safe and familiar.

Patrick's mother had a normal pregnancy and delivery. During his first year he had multiple ear infections, treated with antibiotics. It was discovered he had some moderate hearing loss in his right ear. His language development appeared delayed in this first year. He was babbling by six months and said "Mama" and "Dada," but at one year he lost even that. He lived in his own little world and, as he grew older, began to have temper tantrums. When he became frustrated he would slap his face or bang his head. He played compulsively with cars, taking them apart and refusing to put them back together. In addition to his screaming tantrums, he had spontaneous laughing spells which could last up to an hour. His eye contact was sporadic, and early on he did some finger-flapping. Though his diagnosis, by the age of five-and-a-half, was infantile autism, it was noted by his evaluators that Patrick evidenced "strong potential for learning and development." His autism was considered mild because "he is more communicative, less self-stimulatory, more organized and attentive than more 'classically autistic' children," according to the Developmental Center in Charlottesville.

This prediction proved true, as Patrick, at about eight years of age, began emerging from his solitary world. He began to communicate by talking and became more social and interested in the world around him. He was placed in a public school regular classroom where a special program was developed for his needs. As part of his socialization, "a circle of friends," consisting of his classmates, became partners in his education. When confusion and noise agitated Patrick, these friends would calm themselves down, then chant softly together, "calm down, calm down." Occasionally they would rub his back, accustoming him to purposeful touch. He has become less fearful of change and is slowly learning self-control and to take directions. He has made excellent progress in certain school subjects such as reading and math. Overall, his development in the past few years has been no less than remarkable.

On my way out of the house, I sit with Patrick on the sofa for a few minutes. Here, I get my first taste of his sense of humor and mischievous nature. With a twinkle in his eye, he begins, "Libby, Libby, Libby, on the label, label, label" the song from a commercial. He shows me his cars and talks about the TV program. Interspersed in the logical conversation are silly noises and nonsense words which I learn are a part of his world. I explain what we will be doing in the Dolphin Room. He is immediately interested in the subject of dolphins, showing me a picture book of sea animals. There is a very intelligent little boy underneath all the silliness. He is accepted in his home for all that he is, a charming young man. His verbal skills will be an added help as I begin sessions with the dolphin sounds. He may be able to relate the effects he is experiencing.

So these are the four. Each one unique, each one with a different set of behaviors associated with a disorder that has defied the experts. They represent the wide spectrum of intelligence, manifestations, physical problems, behaviors and frustrations faced by parents and teachers who deal with autism. I have within my little group of four these variables: verbal, nonverbal, male, female, young child, young adult, physically limited, healthy, in school, out of school, and countless others. Shining through their limitations are four wonderful individuals with distinct personalities and potentials for growth in one way or another.

What will the experience be for them? What will it be for me? Will hearing the dolphin's sounds make a positive difference in their lives? Will it be the miracle for which parents hoped? Will all of my theories and hypothesis about the sounds be verified, or will I learn I have been on the wrong path all along? These questions and a myriad of others swirl around in my head as I prepare for the actual sessions in October. There is a part of me that isn't ready to begin. What if it is the end of the whole adventure?

Libby Layne is a little nervous as she begins her study. She thinks that she knows why the sounds make people feel better, but, just like describing eternity, it is going to be very hard to explain. There are scientific facts she has studied that may help, but as we all know, science doesn't know everything. In fact, it sometimes gets in the way of the truth.

I am ready to begin, hoping the time in the Dolphin Room will make a difference for the children who have been sent to me. I am not expecting the dolphin sounds to cure them of their autism.

I have researched extensively the effects of sound vibrations on the human brain. Studies have shown that brain waves pulsate and oscillate at certain frequencies just as sounds do. There are four basic brain wave patterns: Beta Waves, normal waking state; Alpha Waves, daydreaming or states of meditation; Theta Waves, states of high creativity; and Delta Waves, states of deep sleep or unconsciousness. The sound waves which seem to produce an Alpha or meditative and calming state in the brain corresponded to the sound waves produced by dolphin communication.

In his autobiography, Dr. Alfred Tomatis stated that the brain is stimulated by sounds and that one of the primary functions of hearing is this exercising of the brain. It seems to me that if autistic children, for whatever reason, are tuning out the audible world, their brains are not being stimulated and their development is inhibited. He suggests above all else that a listening program of some kind might be of some advantage.

Could there be a sound vibration called DOLFA-WAVE?

I am hoping the sounds might create a "window" into the world where the autistic children of my study live. Through this window, in the safety of the Dolphin Room, the child may allow some light in from my world.

One of the things that concerns me most is my ignorance of "scientific method." Though my study may not be completely scientific, I am determined to keep good records.

Before I visited the children and their parents, I sent a packet to them. It included a form for the child's history and a description of their autistic behaviors, a form asking which behaviors parents would like observed and one to record any changes in behavior at home during the study. I have mounted a video camera on a tripod that will record every minute of every session. Each of these things will help determine whether there is a change in the behaviors of the children when they hear the sounds. I am already aware that there are *way* too many variables for a valid study. There is the room, the sounds outside, the mood of the child, what happened before he came in, what medicine he is taking and probably a hundred others. Since I am not a scientist, I'll not pretend I am; I'll do the best I can with what I know. I suppose I might be called a visionary, believing in more than that which can be proved.

There will be eight sessions with each child, two sessions per week. Each session will last for twenty minutes. When the child comes into the room, the dolphin sounds will begin playing and will end when the session is over. During the time in the Dolphin Room, I will be there to do whatever the child wishes to do — play, talk, sing or just sit. The parents will remain in the room at first, but as soon as is possible, there will be only the child, the dolphin sounds and me.

For the month of October, Libby Layne meets with the children in the Dolphin Room. Each session brings new challenges, new hopes, new questions. The children love the room and are comfortable there. Those who are especially active seem to be calmed by the room and the sounds. Those who aren't affectionate appear to become more affectionate. Those who have language problems seem to communicate better while with Libby Layne in the room. The parents are pleased, even though there are no miracles they can actually see.

That doesn't mean there are no miracles happening!

November, 1994

My study is officially over. The four weeks of regular sessions are ended. I continue working with Dylan and Kim about once a week, using no video but keeping progress notes.

For hours I sit in front of the TV, compiling a tape for each child, representing the eight sessions in sequence. I am encouraged to see positive changes unique to each individual. To make viewing less time-consuming for my experts, I log numbers alongside significant portions which correspond to the numbers on the tape. I make four copies of each child's sessions, and along with the log I compile, pack and mail them to my "experts" who had agreed to review them. I wait anxiously for what, I am positive, will be confirmation of my observations.

Late in January, the pediatrician calls to say she is sending me her evaluation. She asks that, after reading it, I call and discuss her report. Anxious to know at least a positive or negative opinion, I beg, "Please, can't you give me an overall view?"

I am confident that it will be positive. She begins haltingly, in an apologetic voice, perhaps due to our friendship of the past. My heart sinks! When she finishes, it is abundantly clear she has seen no improvement in any of the children's behaviors. She has seen no positive sign that the sounds or what I did in the room had any effect at all. She will send me a copy of her written observations. I almost feel sorry for *her*. She knows how much of myself I have put into this study, the many years leading up to it, and my deep belief in the hypothesis.

"Of course, it's just one opinion from the tapes. You were there, and you have more a feel for what happened."

Little consolation; she was to be my "medical" expert. I know that the medical community is slow to accept anything too innovative concerning autism. I will wait for my other experts.

I call Betsy Smith, who, trying to make me feel better, explains that the pediatrician, coming from a medical model, probably didn't see a change she couldn't explain. She hasn't looked at the tapes, but will in the near future. I then call the AIT practitioner who never returns my calls.

After three months I give up. Neither Betsy nor the AIT practitioner, as far as I know, ever look at the tapes. If they do, they choose not to respond. Here I am with one negative and two no-shows.

Both the parents and I feel that the experience has had positive effects on their children's behaviors. There have been no miracles, but enough positive experiences to continue looking at the possibilities. The result of my study has boiled down to my continuing belief that the sounds are helpful to the children with whom I worked, but there is no way to prove it scientifically. Had I seen only what I wanted to see? Was I blind to the real truth? Yet, had I not been guided to this point? Perhaps there is more to it than I imagine or it is something outside of the realm of science. I will be forced to follow my own gut feeling, my own sense of the truth.

The feeling is a familiar one. Everything is pointing away from what I know in my soul to be true. It had happened before on the Island of Ahousat.

I am pleased with the progress Libby Layne has made through the years. The results of her DOLFA-WAVE study are disappointing and she begins to wonder whether she has misunderstood the meaning of the path she followed for twenty-eight years; **but she just doesn't give up!** *Perhaps she thinks it is time to begin something new. On Ahousat Island she learned to trust herself on the inside, when everything on the outside seemed to be going wrong. Still believing that she has been guided on her dolphin journey, she questions whether the connections she put together are just her own ideas. Does she want them to be true so she can be famous for her amazing discovery? She has also learned to watch out for that "ego trip" trap.*

I find her on her knees at church on Ash Wednesday, preparing for another Lenten season. This is a good place to begin looking.

XI
Chanson

"Behold the might of the New Song! It has made men out of stones, men out of beasts. Those moreover, that were as dead, not being partakers of the true life, have come to life again, simply by becoming listeners to this song. It also composed the universe into melodious order, and tuned the discord of the elements to harmonious arrangement, so that the whole cosmos might become harmony...."

Clement of Alexandria.

February, 1995 Lent

Again I am on my knees looking for guidance as to how best to spend the forty days before Easter. Sometimes I leave it open, and sometimes, like today, I have something specific on my mind.

"Has the dolphin connection been *just* for fun or is it an inseparable part of Some Plan for me?"

I know I have learned many lessons from the dolphins, but perhaps the role they played is not as important as I imagine. From my point of view, this would be fine, but lately I am asked to tell my story to church and school groups. I want to be sure I am telling the *true* story.

I do what humans have done since time began. I ask for a sign.

I had often pondered, "What have the dolphins to do with my Christian faith? Is there a connection?" My answer comes while reading a book called *Jesus Christ, Sun of God* by David Fideler. It tells about the early days of Christianity and some of the symbols they used. I turn the page and see this:

It is an early Christian icon or holy picture. In Greek letters is the secret code that spells "fish" and translates as "Jesus Christ, Son of God, Savior." This code was used in Roman times when Christians were persecuted for their faith. Also on the icon are the Greek letters for Alpha and Omega, the Beginning and the End. And what is the symbol used for Jesus? *A DOLPHIN!* Even before Jesus came to earth, the dolphin was thought to be a sacred animal — "a guide and rescuer of souls." In this icon, the dolphin is used to represent Jesus Christ.

There are times when God works in mysterious ways; at other times, His sign is quite clear. This time He draws a picture; my sign is downright obvious! Now that I am confident there is meaning in the dolphin/God connection, I search for the part sound plays. While reading the book in which I discovered the dolphin icon, I see a quotation from an early Christian leader, Clement of Alexandria. He begins, "Behold the might of the New Song..."

Clement continues, using musical terms like melodious, discord and harmony to connect three things — *The New Song, Jesus Christ* and *The Word* — as one and the same thing. Feeling as if I am on a treasure hunt, searching for something extremely valuable, I look up every reference to *NEW SONG* in the Bible, from Genesis, through the Psalms, to the Revelation in the New Testament. Every passage that includes the phrase "NEW SONG" stresses the importance of praise to the Creator. This is especially true in the Book of Psalms.

I want to burst into singing a Psalm right this very minute, I am so happy for Libby Layne and the discoveries she is making. The connection between the Dolphins and Jesus is exciting and was given to her to let her know she was on the right path. But it is the discovery of the concept of praise that is the important puzzle piece she needs to move forward in her journey.

As angels, we have many duties to perform through eternity. Just look it up sometime. We are, and have always been, very busy. Some of the things we have to do are very serious. But my most favorite thing is singing praises to the Creator God. This is something that we are not required to do; it is simply the most natural way to express our joy. When all of the heavenly hosts join together in praise, it creates such an awesome sound that the vibrations from it reach every corner of the universe. This sound vibration has a very important purpose.

Dolfa-Wave

In the Beginning was a Wave,
And the Wave was with God,
And the Wave was part of God.
And through God
The Wave became flesh
And dwelt among us
And this Wave was called Dolfa.

It manifested itself in many forms
In all of creation,
But its highest vibration
Was in the form of a creature
Which swam in the sea.

This mammal was sleek and smooth
And could streak through the water
At tremendous speed.
This mammal was intelligent
With a brain larger than our own.
It lived in pods of like kind
Where family was of paramount importance.

This creature was there at the beginning,
Millions of years ago
When creation was set into motion
Through the Sound Wave of God.

And still today,
The Sounds this creature makes
Are a reminder of that primal Sound Wave.
They bring us back to our beginnings.

And now abide,
Alpha, Beta, Theta, Delta,
And all other vibrations.
But the vibration
That Sings the New Song,
The vibration that is Praise,
Is DOLFA.

As I continue to read, I realize that in trying to explain mysteries impossible for humans to completely understand, writers of the Bible used words that related to sound. In the Book of Genesis, for instance, the creation of the universe comes about through God's *speaking* it into form.

"Let there be Light.... Let there be sun and moon and stars.... Let there be oceans and land, animals and fish...."

When we think of *speaking,* we think of *sound.* Consider the fact that Jesus is called "The Word" which was there at the beginning, helped create everything, and is part of everything. When we think of *words,* again, we naturally think of *sound.* No matter what you believe about how or when the universe was created, it is no accident that these particular words were used.

Throughout the Bible, everything that is created is asked to praise: "sun and moon, shining stars, wild animals, flying birds, fire and hail, fruit trees and cedars, young men and women, old and young together; *let all creation praise God."* (Psalm 148) Praise can be expressed at any time, any place, with our voices or with instruments like trumpets, or harps, or cymbals. I wonder why this is so important?

This is the question I ponder as I consider the concept of praise and its connection to what I do with dolphin sounds and autistic children. I still believe the sounds the dolphins make are unique in the animal kingdom and somehow make people feel better. I know that when I swim with the dolphins, I can feel the vibrations in my body, and afterwards I am changed for the better in many ways. Dolphins have been on the earth in their present form for at least 40,000,000 years. Most likely they have been making their sounds for that long too. So what did that have to do with praise and the New Song?

I haven't put it all together yet, but I decide one important thing. The connections I *have* put together — sound, vibration, praise, New Song and The Word — are enough to let me know I am on the right path.

The Fifth Day

God's Time
May not be marked as our own.
But whenever the Fifth Day was
In God's Time,
Dolphins were created.
Praise be to God for the Fifth Day

Dolphinswim 1995

As I begin this year's trip, I feel an even greater sense of anticipation than usual. The discovery of the Dolphin icon and New Song give a fresh perspective to my swim. Connections I have made throughout the years have fallen into some semblance of order. Something new may develop in my work with dolphin sounds, even though DOLFA-WAVE seems to have moved to the background.

For the first time, I will stay for two weeks. The anxiety, as to whether or not the dolphins come, is greatly diminished. They will surely come.

A new angle has been added to this trip, one I am not sure I like. There are children, young children, on board, members of a family from Boulder, Colorado. The older, about eight, reminds me of my granddaughter, Sarah; the younger is five. It becomes apparent at the opening night circle that the parents expect all of us to help watch the girls, sort of a throwback to the 60's commune mentality. I make it clear I don't take the responsibility of my *own* grandchildren around water and certainly would not do so with someone else's children. It is nerve-racking as they totter about the boat. One slip of a foot would send them overboard into the ocean. They are well-behaved, and as long as they don't ask me to be responsible, I'll deal with it.

My cabin mate is a lovely Englishwoman with an outrageous sense of humor. She constantly uses Cockney-English twists of language which she must then explain because they are so obscure. She is writing a book about her family, which she describes as "completely mad." Delphine Starr, the Englishwoman from my first Dolphin swim is here and will stay on next week to be joined by her two daughters.

The facilitators on both trips are called "animal communicators," whatever that means! There will be a different one each week, and I have promised myself to remain open-minded. Another exposure to the world of "woo-woo."

The water is extremely rough, and getting on and off the platform is treacherous. The dolphins are numerous, but not wanting to get injured and spoil the entire trip, I don't go in at first. After a few days, the sea calms and I have some wonderful encounters. My swimming and diving have improved greatly over the years, and I have learned how to make the most of each encounter. Having given up the desire to be in the trip video allows me the opportunity to just be with the dolphins where they are.

The "animal communicator" begins her first session by giving us an exercise in telepathy. I have given myself permission to go "ultra-woo-woo" if I wish on this trip, to experience everything fully. The first night we are asked to "think" a shade of the color pink. As we concentrate, our partner tries to pick up the message. I decide on "Pepto-Bismol Pink" and visualize it coating the stomach as in the commercials. My partner immediately receives the message and describes what I had visualized perfectly. Later I am the receiver and don't do well at all — a reminder I need to be more open to other people's messages, perhaps?

As the week progresses, I am less and less impressed with the facilitator. She has an extremely negative attitude and dislikes men. It occurs to me that the reason for her attachment to animals may be her inability to communicate with humans. Her "profession" — communicating with animals — becomes suspect as she confidently claims to know when, where, how and why the dolphins do or do not appear. I quietly withdraw from her sessions for the remainder of the week.

Being out of the mainstream gives me an opportunity to be with Rebecca more than I have on previous trips. She is always so gracious to everyone and shares her time with all the guests. During the time we spend together, our friendship reaches a new level of intimacy as we discuss our spiritual beliefs and find we share a mutual understanding.

As the week continues, the varied individuals on board become like family. The children are a joy and add an extra childlike quality to the overall experience. Their father plays the mandolin, and at the closing circle we perform an arrangement of my song "The Bliss." This group, as on the other trips, identifies with the sentiments in the song and is grateful someone has expressed them in this way.

The second week begins with an entirely new group, except for Delphine who is joined by her daughters. She will be my cabin mate. During the first week we had begun to discuss her philosophy of life, which comes predominantly from New Age teachings. I shared with her my Christian perspective that had been enhanced by this philosophy. I look forward to continuing our discussions.

We have a new animal communicator who is more negative than the first. I make a decision quickly that I will not attend her sessions and, in a nice way, explain I have had enough group encounters the week before. She is very gracious, and I am free to do what I like.

Again this week we have children — two eleven-year-old boys. They are well-behaved, but they *are* boys and change the atmosphere of tranquility somewhat. Every group's energy is different, and this one is no exception. It is less cohesive than last week. Again, with an international guest list, there are some language barriers; there are also some personal ones.

Delphine and I have wonderful and lengthy discussions which include our completely different upbringing. I share with her my growing up on a farm, my large, close family. In her most posh English accent she comments, "Libby, I've never met anyone with such a *staggeringly stable* family!" She also comments that she has rarely heard a Christian speak as I do. She finds it refreshing to hear that someone can be completely committed to a Christian theology, yet remain so non-judgemental, so open-minded.

Rebecca and I also continue our conversations of a spiritual nature and come to the subject of praise and thanksgiving. Out of the dolphin experience, we agree, comes a profound sense of thanksgiving, leading to a natural and spontaneous praise of the Creator God. In our early years, each of us had experienced the power of psalms in the Bible. The praise of God in all situations, "in all things," seems to both of us, an essential component of a fulfilling life. I share my discovery of the Dolphin icon and New Song, explaining my concept of the importance of psalms as a sound vibration of praise. The vibration of praise is contagious.

As we expand this concept, an idea begins to form. If praise is so important and such a natural part of my own life, why can't I write psalms of my own, based on everyday life, everyday situations. After all, that's what "The Bliss" is all about: a thanksgiving for the dolphin experience. I certainly have felt grateful for many other experiences in my life. These modern day psalms might encourage others to give thanks, to shout praises, to "sing a New Song." Could this be my part in moving others to, as Clement of Alexandria said, "Behold the might of the New Song... so that the whole world might become harmony"? I can hardly wait to begin.

Toward the end of the week, the winds finally calm and the day is beautiful; the water is mirrorlike as it shimmers in the sun. A large group of dolphins comes and stays for hours. They are in a very lethargic mood, gliding through the water effortlessly at our sides. Gone is the frolicking mood they exhibit in rough seas.

It is easy to lose track not only of time, but of space when swimming with the dolphins. I find myself with two other people and six or eight dolphins quite far from the boat. Time is suspended as a mother and baby swim quietly at my side for a seemingly endless time. It is so intimate, so intentional, so dear. There is no camera to record this magical time, but the film in my heart and soul record for all time the encounter for which I had wished since beginning my journey. It is truly Bliss!

As this trip ends, I go home to begin a new chapter of my dolphin journey, the writing of a book of psalms: *The New Song; Psalms for the Next Millennium.*

There she goes again, positive she's figured it all out. It always amuses me, after one of her Epiphanies, seeing Libby Layne leap to a conclusion exclaiming, "this is IT!" I love her for it, of course; this is the way she learns. It also warms my heart watching her bubbling enthusiasm.

Did you know the word enthusiastic comes from the Greek, meaning "inspired by God"?

When she returns from her spring dolphin swim, she is ready to write her book of psalms. Her inspirations come from various daily experiences and activities, a news report, a family interaction, conversation with a friend, a dream, or a memory. Many times the ideas float into her mind as she takes her walks. A two-week trip to Europe with her community choir gives her some beautiful experiences from which to write. She fills notebooks with thoughts and ideas that come into her head. In the fall she spends a week all alone in her parents' place at the beach, composing psalms from her notes. She finds that the lines of each psalm come to her in pieces, not necessarily in order. She learns to write them down as they come to her, reworking them again and again. She always knows, somehow, when they are finished. It's almost as if they were already composed somewhere else, that she is merely writing them down. She becomes aware that she is a voice through which someone else is singing. At the end of the week she has written thirty psalms.

One of the first she wrote is "Of Grace and Daisies," a reflection on her rape experience. A minister friend of hers had told of this experience in one of his books. Thinking he might be interested, she sends him the psalm. She also mentions her idea of publishing a book called The New Song; Psalms for the Next Millennium *someday. His response is positive, both to the psalm and the idea of the book. He suggests that she send what she has already written to several publishers right away. It is difficult, he says, for an unpublished author to find a publisher; it takes time. He gives her names and addresses of several and permission to use his name when she writes to one with whom he has worked. He believes the story behind the psalms is an unusual one and suggests she include an essay along with the psalms. The story of her journey with the dolphins might attract special attention.*

She and Harry are preparing for another RV trip; they will be gone for three months starting in January. Wanting to get something in the mail before they leave, she prints out the psalms she believes are best and writes an essay about her dolphin adventures and her work with autistic children and sound.

Her daughter, the artist, draws some beautiful illustrations which are added to the manuscript. The psalms, essay, illustrations and a cover letter are assembled and sent to each of eight publishers.

Friends and family who have read the psalms think they are wonderful and are certain someone will want to publish them. These people may be somewhat prejudiced because they love her, but she has high hopes. After all, she has been guided to write the psalms, hasn't she?

It can sometimes take months for manuscripts to be read. As they leave for their trip, Libby Layne asks the house sitter to call if any mail comes from a publisher. Her minister friend has said that if she wants her manuscript returned, she should send a self-addressed, stamped envelope. She is confident at least one publisher will be thrilled to have the chance to publish her book, maybe more! (I do love her optimism. It is a rare thing. I wish there were more of it.)

One by one, her manuscripts are returned, some with little handwritten comments . Some say, "we don't publish poetry"; some are just form letters saying "thanks but no thanks." She learns that very few publishing companies are interested in poetry, especially poetry of an unknown and unpublished author. Encouraged by some of the com-

ments on the returned manuscripts, she sends them back out to others. She is in no hurry and knows this could be a long process.

After six months of rejections, one of the last comments is especially intriguing. "We find we are more interested in your work with the dolphins and the autistic children. That's really wonderful. Why don't you write that up someday?"

We'll join Libby Layne on her latest Dolphinswim trip as she begins to write her story.

XII
Theme and Variations II

Dolphinswim, 1996
Friday, 12:30 PM

Thankfully, my Charlotte connection really *has* been held for me. After running full speed through the airport, I leap on the plane beneath my marginally legal carry-ons, launching into an explanation of my luggage situation, "The reason I am carrying all this stuff and not checking it, is because I'm going to swim with the dolphins and my fins and snorkel are in the carry-ons and I'm afraid they might get lost and I don't have time to find them before I get on the boat in the morning," I babble on and on like the proverbial brook. Politely quieting my gabble, the attendant ushers me to my seat as another helpful attendant hoists the two heavy bags into the overhead compartment. Relieved, I sit down in the last seat on board and the plane takes off to Ft. Lauderdale, right on schedule.

The attendant arrives at my seat with the drink cart. Leaning over, she remarks excitedly, "I'm moving to a new house this week and it's on *Dolphin* Street." There are always questions stimulated by the mention of dolphins or my wardrobe of dolphin T-shirts and jewelry. The fascination with these wonderful creatures is universal, and I always enjoy sharing my experiences when asked. (Even when I'm not asked!) The young man seated next to me joins the conversation. Where, he asks, might he take his wife to swim with dolphins for their anniversary? A year before, she had an encounter with dolphins and couldn't stop talking about it. On the back of my DOLFA-WAVE business card, I write the names of several swim programs with wild dolphins. Who knows what will happen to that girl who has been lured into the dolphin's world, just as I was twenty-eight years ago?

Friday, 2:35 PM

In Ft. Lauderdale I board the twenty-passenger prop plane taking me to Freeport. In only thirty minutes I'll be near the *Sea Fever,* my equipment safe, and when visual contact is made with Rebecca, I can finally relax.

The weather is beautiful as we circle Ft. Lauderdale, flying over the aqua blue water of the Atlantic on our way to the even bluer water near the Bahamas. The flight is smooth and short, with only time for a Diet Coke.

The ten passengers fill out customs forms in preparation to land at the tiny tropical pink Freeport Airport. After landing, we go inside the terminal where we line up to get our passports stamped.

"How long will you be here?" the entry officer asks. "Where will you be staying? Is this business or pleasure?"

Every year I expect to have my entry rejected for some unknown international offense. The officer stamps my passport and smiles, "Have a nice stay."

Outside, I hail a taxi to the hotel where I will stay until the boat departure in the morning. This year I am staying at a new hotel, the Port Lucayan. It was the Lucayan Resort Hotel last year. Or is it the other way around?

The taxi takes me directly to the Port Lucayan where I know exactly how much to pay the driver. Five years ago, coming here for the first time, I worried I might be overcharged or taken for a ride around the island. Today I am confident, having learned the Bahamians are gentle, honest people, happy to see tourists.

I check in at the Port Lucayan Resort. They have my reservation in the computer under Dolphinswim — group rate. The right place, the right day, the right time. Now where is Rebecca?!

Friday, 6:00 PM

Settled in the hotel, I ring Rebecca's room. Her familiar, cheerful voice on the other end of the line finally erases any remaining anxiety. Dolphinswim 1996 is going to happen!

On the night before departure, Dolphinswim participants go to dinner at one of the cafes in Lucayan Market Square. My only knowledge of these people is a list of names and addresses, sent by Rebecca before the trip.

Meeting us in the lobby of the hotel, Rebecca makes the introductions. There is an English family: mother, father, and two young girls. The younger has won a children's lottery — the prize, a Dolphinswim trip for her and her sister. Both too young to come alone, the parents have accompanied them. There is another young English girl, who will be my cabin mate, and a woman from Alaska. Then, there are the Japanese: Sagako, Suwako, Yoshiro, Noriko, Kazuko, and Shingo. Should be an interesting week trying to keep *those* names straight! Horace Dobbs, with whom I went on my first Dolphinswim, will join us, but has not arrived from England.

There are many questions about what to expect as we walk to the restaurant. Other than Rebecca, I am the only one who has been on a previous trip. Our common passion, the dolphins, bridges our diverse backgrounds as we begin to become acquainted. Though now complete strangers, these individuals will, in six short days, bond together in the unique way only a dolphin swim experience can provide. In a sense, we become a human pod.

After dinner and conversation, the group disperses, drifting separately into different corners of the market square. Rebecca and I walk together to the hotel, renewing our friendship of previous years.

With the anticipation of a child on Christmas Eve, I crawl into bed, hoping sleep will come quickly. Visions of Sugar Plums are replaced by dreams of dolphins, the dawn bringing promise of precious gifts.

The Dramamine I have taken to jump-start the seasick medicine in my system makes me drowsy. I offer a prayer of thanks for this opportunity, allowed me year after year. As I fall asleep, I also give thanks for the journey, with all of its connections and coincidences, that have brought me here.

Day 1, 8:00 AM

After breakfast, we gather in the lobby, this time accompanied by our luggage and diving gear. We are met by two crew members from the *Sea Fever* who load it on a dolly, then take it to where the boat is docked nearby.

Horace Dobbs, who has arrived during the night, jovially greets me with, "Hullo, Libby Layne." It was he, on my first Dolphinswim trip four years ago, who encouraged me to take back my little girl name. I look forward to hearing about his work and play with the dolphins in the interim. He will be, as he was four years ago, the facilitator on this trip. He is without Dr. Nakagawa and his entourage, but his work in Japan has drawn many Japanese on this trip.

We step aboard the *Sea Fever,* a large blue and white diving boat chartered for the trip. Captain Tom has been skipper on each of my previous trips; the crew is always different. This year, Renee will Captain and Liz returns as chef. As usual, the young men who crew are helpful and friendly as they guide us and our gear to our quarters below.

I am assigned to one of the nicest and most spacious staterooms on the boat. In this case, both *spacious* and *stateroom* are relative terms, meaning there are only two people in the cabin and the sink is in the closet rather than out in the hall. It does not mean, however, that the two people can dress at the same time. My English cabin mate, Frances, and I unpack — one at a time — then go up to the lounge, where the safety talk soon begins.

Captain Renee and crew members in turn recite their part of the safety information, the location of life preservers and how to use vital equipment on board.

"Put nothing in the 'head' that hasn't first gone in your mouth."

"Do *not* inflate the life boats on the upper deck; it costs $1000 to repack them."

"Seasick medicine won't work after you're already sick."

"Breakfast is served at 7:00 AM, lunch at 1:00 PM, dinner at 7:00 PM. Of course if the dolphins come, they take precedence."

After signing our lives away on release forms, the motors roar into action and we're on our way. The trip to the open sea takes about five hours — two to the West End of Grand Bahama Island, then three more hours to where the dolphins are. It isn't likely we'll see dolphins until we're out farther, but there's always the chance! We don bathing suits, climb the ladder to the upper deck and stare into the blue clear waters, waiting for the cry, "Dolphins on the Bow!"

3:00 PM

The water is changing from a deep navy blue to the brilliant Caribbean aqua-blue-green, a sign we are nearing the more shallow Bahama Banks where the Spotted Dolphins swim. While having snorkel practice earlier at the West End of Grand Bahama Island, we saw several Bottlenose Dolphins feeding. They were intent on their activity and could not be enticed into a ride on the bow wave. It was enough, however, to excite everyone on board. There *were* dolphins out here!

We begin looking in earnest. They usually appear on the bow wave at the South Bank, the North Bank or somewhere in between. We're awfully early this year. Will they be around, ready to play? Anticipation mounts. The air is chilly, as is the water. I am glad I brought a wet suit.

I go to the upper deck where bodies are already baking in the sun. The Japanese man, Yoshiro (I think), has on a full body suit of some kind but is oblivious to the heat as he and others have been driven to naps by the Dramamine.

I'm ready anytime now! I scan the ocean. Nothing but blue as far as I can see. Three hundred and sixty degrees of blue, broken only by small whitecaps bubbling up in the water and puffy white clouds drifting in the sky.

Sometimes they hear us coming. They remember the sound of the motor and can distinguish between the *Sea Fever*, the *Stenella* or the *Dream Time*. I'm not surprised. Their memory for sound is acute. They know each other by their individual signature whistle. I wonder if they'll remember my signature sound this year.

The Flood
Where did the Dolphins go during The Flood?
Most likely they rode the bow wave of the Ark,
And entertained everyone on board,
Just like today.

5:00 PM

"I don't feel them around, do you?" Rebecca remarks.

"Maybe tomorrow," I answer.

We have remained all day in the same general area, with no sign of the dolphins. The water is shallow, about thirty feet. At this depth, sizable waves, caused by the increased winds, constantly toss the boat up and down. Those whose systems aren't yet adjusted to sea living are looking a bit green. For the comfort of everyone aboard, we prepare to move to deeper and calmer water where we will have dinner and spend the night. The anchor is raised, the engines roar, and the boat accelerates.

As the bow wave forms, we suddenly hear the much-awaited cry, "Dolphins on the bow!"

Racing forward, Rebecca takes up her ritual shrieking, followed by the rest of us, converging on the narrow port and starboard decks. Hanging over the rail of the bow, butts in the air, we pound the hull, whistling and screaming with delight. The humans are now having their first training session with the dolphins. This scene will be enacted each and every time the dolphins appear for the next week, as if we had gone to obedience school. I always imagine that the wild dolphins experience an enjoyment similar to humans, watching as captive dolphins go through their series of trained maneuvers. Here, we are the captives, they the trainers. We perform perfectly and right on schedule.

They always seem excited at our arrival, especially the first week. Frances is surprised by her reaction, as tears spring to her eyes. "I didn't know I would do this just seeing them," she whispers. They beckon us to come in, but not too soon — they want that ride on the bow first.

Everyone begins donning gear. Wet suits are tugged over sweaty bodies. We spit into masks, rinsing them in the appropriate fresh water barrel. Cameras are checked for film and hung around necks. For beginners, snorkel vests are distributed. With fins clumsily flopping across the deck, we line up like a flock of mismatched ducks, waiting for the call from a crew member, "Dive, Dive, Dive!" I don't hurry, having learned that if the dolphins decide to stay, there will be plenty of time. Newcomers fidget impatiently at the railing.

The engine is put into neutral, the restraining rope is unhooked, and we finally hear, "Dive, Dive, Dive!"

One by one we drop ten or twelve feet from the boat's starboard side to the surface of the water where the dolphins wait. Only for a moment do I notice the chilliness of the water, as I am immediately greeted by a familiar pair — the mother and baby who last year shared with me the encounter of a lifetime. For over an hour we had swum together in an intensely intimate experience.

For the first time, I feel there is recognition between the dolphins and me. Though other return swimmers have related tales of meeting "old friends," I have never experienced it. Through my mask, I make my "signature sound" as we renew our friendship in a chorus of sonics and mutual joy.

The dolphins dive in and out among the swimmers, scanning them with their sonar as if to determine what manner of guests they will entertain this week. After this initial welcome, the ten dolphins of various ages stay for over an hour, hosting a gala encounter.

Then, one by one, our hosts disappear into the vast ocean. We never know when they will appear again or what influences their stay. When they choose to remain with us, we are overcome by a sense of wonder and are profoundly grateful for their hospitality.

The exhausted party guests return to the boat, each excitedly relating his or her personal experience. Seeing new faces with the afterglow of a first encounter is always a personal joy for me. When everyone is out of the water, several dolphins return and linger near the boat, seeming to want more play. It is tempting, but everyone is tired and hungry. Dinner has already been held for an hour, a fairly regular event as dolphins take priority even over Liz's gourmet cooking.

Tonight we will have "opening circle" on the upper deck under the stars. Participants will introduce themselves and have an opportunity to explain what led them to this experience. Horace will give a little talk, and more than likely, everyone will turn in early. I know I will. What a *great* first day!

Day 2, 6:00 AM

Something is changing; I feel it! I am alone on deck. Only two people are stirring below: the crew person who had watch last night and Liz who has put coffee and tea out for the early birds.

As the sun rises over an ocean of salty water, salty tears stream down my face. No particular reason; I simply feel full to running over with the beauty of what this trip means. Oddly, I don't yet know what that is.

I replay last night's opening circle — a special one. On six previous first nights, I have participated in this ritual. Though on each trip the people are completely different, similar are their reasons for wanting to be on a boat in the middle of the ocean, waiting to swim with dolphins.

Barely audible above the generator, the Japanese begin to speak. As Orientals often do, they bring a grace and elegance to the atmosphere. Some share their abiding dream of swimming with dolphins, a familiar theme. They speak of learning, receiving healing, and having their lives changed. Some speak English well, while others are helped by friends who translate for them. One of those who barely speaks English is Yoshiro, an older man. He has come, although reluctantly, because his eighteen-year-old daughter insisted. Beginning in halting Japanese, then through a translator, he tells us of his difficulty with relationships and talking with people, even at home. He knows only a few English words, he says, but expresses his desire to communicate with all of us. Without knowing precisely why, this touches me deeply. Perhaps Yoshiro's plight is similar to that of a person with autism, living in an isolated world where communication is a barrier instead of a bridge. We who have been given this bridge as a gift and to whom it is natural and easy must find new ways of reaching those who don't have this gift. One of the lessons dolphins teach is that there are many ways to communicate.

Then tiny Noriko, Yoshiro's daughter, speaks. The only words she manages before bowing her head in tears are, "This is a dream come true." Kazuko, one of the older girls, goes to comfort her and translates further, "I love being here with you; I am so lucky."

As spokesman for his family, David, the English father, tells us this is the first time any of them have traveled from their home. In his Bromley, Kent accent he confesses he has been "closed up" for many years and feels this will be a new beginning for his family and his relationship with them.

As others tell diverse but equally touching stories, the mood of the group is quiet, receptive and very sweet. We have come full circle to Rebecca. Silence ... more silence.

"Well, this is a first," she finally begins, gaining her composure through tears born of an intense emotion, shared by all. She relates, in a hushed voice, her personal journey involving the dolphins. I have heard this fascinating tale many times, but in this telling there is a difference. It isn't so much *what* she says as *how* she says it. As she speaks, there is a profound reverence, a sense of the sacred.

"What the dolphins have, we have within us; they just remind us of it."

There is silence. Each one in the group assimilates what has gone before and waits for Horace to speak. On these occasions he usually takes the opportunity to speak of his work and introduces what he will teach during the trip as a facilitator. Tonight he, too, seems touched by the poignancy of the moment. He says that as a child in England during World War II, he was taught to hate the Japanese. His work with dolphins in recent years has exposed him to many wonderful Japanese who share a common interest in learning what the dolphins have to teach. This association has caused a profound change in his attitude. He speaks of acceptance rather than prejudice, that this is a key in changing the world for the better.

Teachers of the Sea

Hanging over the bow
Whistling, screaming, shouting
at these sea mammals,
People all over the world gather,
Fascinated.
Since the early days
Of creation
They've been with us,
Inspiring stories of rescue,
Teasing us with their intelligence,
Seeking us out in the blue waters.
We have
Hunted them,
Captured them,
Killed them.
Yet they keep coming to us in Love,
Showing us how families stay together,
Showing us how to care for each other,
Reminding us of the joy of play,
Reminding us that pollution kills,
Revealing to us the wonder of the brain,
Revealing to us that there are many ways to communicate,
Helping us to Remember our Origins
In God.

9:30 AM

The boat is moving northward. When underway, there is always a possibility that the motor noise and the wake of the boat will attract the dolphins. Not this time.

We anchor over The Light Structure, a sunken light buoy teeming with beautiful sea plants and water creatures. Several people brave the cold, rough water but are soon driven back on board. Unless there are dolphins, I generally avoid these sea conditions.

Small groups gather here and there talking. Several of the Japanese sit silently, eyes closed in meditation.

With a lull in activity, Rebecca and I go below to my cabin for a quiet visit. We continue our discussion of last year, sharing our feelings of reverence and praise we experience in our association with the dolphins. We are aware of our profound sense of thanksgiving for the gift of this trip, year after year. This natural expression of joy and wonder, we feel, is an essential component of worship of the Creator God. The Japanese have a word for it, *Arigato,* meaning "being thankful in all things."

I am still fascinated by the connection between the dolphin's communication sounds and the concept of praise. Years ago at the school I helped start, the power of the Humpback whalesong was to change the lives of teachers and students, as well as my own. The call of the sea mammals was faint then. I was not yet aware I was being enchanted by their song. Unlike the music of the sea sirens luring sailors to their deaths, these sounds were leading me to LIFE.

12:00 Noon

We're moving again. The sound of the motors combined with the imminent serving of lunch is a condition frequently chosen by the dolphins for an appearance. We've seen only one dolphin, an uninterested, lone Bottlenose, all morning.

"Dolphin on the bow, lunch is served!"

It's happened again!

2:30 PM

The earlier was a false alarm — the dolphin part, at least. We did have lunch. Giving in to a Dramamine stupor and a bountiful lunch, I curl up with pillow and blanket for a rest on one of the booth benches in the lounge. Others are swimming in water still too cool and rough for my taste. I have the luxury of two weeks to pace my swimming activities. There is no hurry or worry that I'm wasting time doing nothing. On a trip such as this, doing nothing is doing something wonderful. What a shame I don't carry this attitude into life at home as well.

In response to both my upbringing and the puritan "work" ethic, my focus has always been "to do" and "to do the right thing." After a half-century of voluntarism, I have become aware that being involved, in even the most philanthropic of activities, can be a trap for my ego — *I Am,* because *I Do.* I have gone in and out of this trap throughout my life, learning repeatedly that who I am comes from a source independent of what I do. Still, each time the trap is baited, I step into it willingly, getting caught, unaware. Only later do I realize I am snared again, trying to prove my worthiness in this wonderful life, trying somehow to repay the blessings I have been given. I am reminded of how little I understood grace until that fateful walk in September of 1988.

How much more I find there is to learn.

5:00 PM

Almost the end of the day and still no dolphins. We're at the South Sandbar, and if they don't appear soon, we'll begin moving north as we did yesterday. A brisk north wind continues to churn the ocean into sizable waves. A report from Skipper Renee's radio promises a calming trend tomorrow. We're all ready for *that.* Several people have gotten actively seasick, while others have managed to sleep it off with the help of Dramamine. I haven't had a bout with it since my first trip but always keep some prevention in my system just in case. Salsa and chips still settle my stomach!

Today is Sunday, and I recall a comment made by Captain Tom last year concerning the frequency of dolphin no-shows on this day. He guessed that if he checked the log book in past years he would find a high incidence of Sundays being dolphin-less. A believer in such "un-coincidences," I wondered if this were the case. Perhaps they are reminding us of the sacredness of this day. That seems to be stretching a point, however, as Friday sundown to Saturday sundown is sacred to Jews, and other belief systems have their own holy days. Could it be they remind us that every day is sacred and holy?

I am always amused when we humans attempt to read the dolphin mind: why they come to swim or not, why they stay or not, why they do anything they do. It is tempting to mystify these wonderful creatures of nature. "They are aliens, they are angels, they are guides, they are gurus, they are gods," we surmise. Just what or who they are is a mystery, and I find myself going back and forth between my rational knowledge of a sea mammal and my personal experience of the dolphins being more than just wild creatures. Do they really communicate telepathically? My first experience with a wild dolphin at Virginia Beach led me to believe that they do.

6:00 PM

The second full day has ended with no appearances by dolphins, yet there have been no complaints from this group. We agreeably accept it, using the time to become better acquainted with each other, reading or going swimming in the crystal clear waters.

Frances and I are becoming close. A special bond is being forged in only a short time based on a common situation, the mother/daughter relationship. She is having problems with her mother, I with my daughter who is the same age as she. In our conversations, I am, at times, the mother she doesn't have; at other times I confide in her as if she were a daughter who understands my pain. She has also been deeply hurt by the institutional Christian church. In giving up the faith of her youth, she is somewhat lost as she searches for something in which to believe. Like many on these trips, she has been drawn to New Age thought. Many Christian churches fail to meet the spiritual needs of a changing society, and people have been leaving the church in great numbers. Taking a somewhat broader view of the Christian message, I have enjoyed challenging these people to rethink what this message might be. By feeling free to explore various religions and philosophies, I have assimilated them without compromising my basic Christian beliefs. The traditional message has been so distorted over time that it no longer is relevant to many people. It is no longer "The Good News."

Later, as we wait for dinner, Rebecca and I discuss the future of Dolphinswim and the new boat she and her husband plan to buy. She explains her desire to create an atmosphere of reverence, a sense of the sacred on the trips. I am reminded of our school and the dream we had for the same ambience there. I still feel some disappointment that it did not work out as some of us had planned.

As we go in to have dessert, continuing our discussion, I notice crew members going about their duties in the galley, cleaning up dinner dishes and setting up for breakfast. I am reminded of the retreat I made to the Carmelite Monastery in Nova Scotia years ago. The time I spent there heightened my awareness of the sacredness of everyday tasks: washing dishes, making a bed, opening a can of beans, or sweeping the floor. Each act became a holy one. As I recall this experience, I share it with Rebecca. We agree that this could be the atmosphere on the new boat. We could share duties of cooking and cleaning, encouraging community and a sense of brotherhood. There would be meditation and a sense of thanksgiving and praise.

Day 3, 10:30 AM

The boat is headed to more sheltered waters. Last night we rocked *considerably* more than was necessary to put us to sleep. People are beginning to look a little peaked again as we sway almost horizontal to the ocean. Still we have no dolphins.

As we take the extremely rough ride nearer land, Suwako is doing Japanese massage on Fran who is feeling queasy. Yesterday, after writing for two days, my hand was really feeling the stress. Suwako offered the gift of her healing hands, and her touch was a welcome relief. As a thank-you, I sang *The Bliss*. It is always a joy sharing my experience through music with others having their own dolphin experience.

Listening with eyes closed, she mused, "I see pictures of dolphins dancing."

Though she missed many of the lyrics, she understood the soul of the song. Regardless of language or culture, everyone seems to relate to its meaning.

We arrive near the beach of a little island called Sandy Cove where we finally get relief from the rough seas and wind. It is a privately owned island, inhabited by an old Bahamian man who doesn't mind visitors. After anchoring, small groups are taken by inflatable boat to its shore. Before our group goes to the island, we explore the recent wreckage of a freighter, discovering that its sinking is too recent to have attracted sea life — there is little to see but a rusty hull. We swim there for a short time, then go to the island where we look for shells and enjoy "terra firma."

The old man of the island does not appear, though evidence of his simple life there does; on the beach is a large circle of conch shells, placed strategically to catch fish when the tide comes in.

While walking the shore with the teenager from England, we spy a pink toilet sitting upright in the sand. As we approach the commode, I fabricate a zany story about how it came to be there. As children, my sisters and I would find an object such as this and invent magical stories which eventually became legend in our family. She gave me one of those teenage looks, quietly listening as I spun the yarn. I wondered whether she thought I was a bit daft, but by the time we returned to the big boat, her entire family knew the story. The pink toilet was immortalized!

With everyone feeling better having been on land, we brave the rougher seas searching for dolphins, hoping they will grant us audience. This is such a patient group that never complains, though for two days we have seen only fleeting glances of our ocean friends. Several appear on the bow, then on the stern, then they are gone. Though I have the luxury of another week, I find myself anxious for the others who have only five more days.

Taking up my vigil on the upper deck, scanning the water for a fin, I am reminded of the family trip to Virginia Beach. Sitting for days, gazing out to sea, I had waited for the return of my first dolphin friend from earlier that spring. My determination had paid off.

Day 4, 8:00 AM

The seas are much calmer today, certainly more calm than last night. The wind blew us back and forth so forcefully that the slap of the water on the bottom of the boat kept me awake half the night. I foresee a nap in my future.

This would be a perfect day for a long encounter, and these people deserve it. I offer a very specific prayer, "Please send the dolphins!"

1:00 PM

The ocean appears as a smooth lake. The wind has completely calmed, not a wave in sight, and the sun is intense. Lunch has been served and devoured. Liz did it again: Chicken Caesar salad, ambrosia and homemade bread! It's a good thing we get plenty of exercise, the way we are being fed. The sea air deludes the body into a false notion that survival is dependent on three full meals a day, snacks and dessert. Naps *are* essential, so I snuggle into a bunk with my blanket and pillow.

2:00 PM

Everyone is going in for a swim. Those who are adventurous ride "The Wild Thing," a rubber inner-tube pulled by the inflatable Zodiak boat. It whizzes around the big boat, the rider frantically grasping the rubber handles and hanging on for dear life. Others begin jumping off the highest deck of the boat. Applause! Applause!

"Come on Libby, jump off the boat," they taunt. This kind of applause I *don't* need. As a kid I allowed myself to be intimidated into jumping off the high board, hating every minute. But not today; age does have its compensations.

The water finally lures me in, and I have an inspiration — Water Ballet!

"Come on Rebecca, it's showtime!" I yell. Cathy, Lois and Frances join the troupe. I am choreographer, as our audience gathers on board, video cameras rolling.

"O.K. ladies, make a circle, feet in the center. On an eight count kick your feet as we move apart; then do a back flip. Keep your toes pointed! Ready? One, Two, Three..." Esther Williams, eat your heart out! Of course, three-quarters of the people on board are too young to have ever heard of Esther Williams!

All right, we've all been patient, have busied ourselves and not complained, pretending we're completely satisfied with things as they are. But time is running out. WE WANT DOLPHINS!

3:30 PM

Everyone is curious about my writing, the word circulating that it might be a book someday. I have certainly had plenty of time with the dolphin situation as it is. I'd gladly give up a little writing time if...

"Dolphins on the Bow!" comes the long anticipated cry. As we dash to the bow, we count three, four, six, NINE dolphins. After our retraining session with the dolphins at the bow, we scramble to get on the ever-tight wet suits and other clumsy gear. Everyone gets in the water, positive this will be one like the first day. The water is perfect, and we expect the dolphins to stay around.

The dolphins weave in and out of the swimmers quickly, as if checking to see who is there, then they are gone. I barely see them as they move away. Everyone gets back on board, disappointed but encouraged that we've been near them again, at least for a moment.

As soon as we start moving again, they are back; this time there are six of them. For some reason, I feel compelled to stay on board. I had several beautiful encounters the first day and have another week ahead of me. Fifteen others wait to go in again, having only this week. If swimmers outnumber dolphins, the dolphins tend to leave quickly, especially mothers with new calves. I learned this lesson during my first organized swim on the research vessel. I have developed a profound respect for the dolphin's space.

"This is *their* home," the researcher had said, "*we* are the guests here."

My instinct to stay out of the water for this particular encounter is a good one. Watching from the deck, I see that three dolphins have surrounded Frances. As if knowing how badly she needs a special encounter, they appear to swim to her intentionally.

I watch for a time as Frances has her encounter, enjoying it as if it were my own. Later I go in the water and observe as the dolphins do their ballet among the swimmers. They are so generous with everyone, giving each individual a special memory. Bringing their babies, the mothers allow them to play with the humans, somehow comfortable that they will not be harmed. The dolphins seem to know the energy of the group and respond to it. This group of people is also generous in nature, by far the most sensitive group with whom I have been on any swim.

As we return to the boat, sharing with tears and laughter our individual encounters, I see Frances with a rather bewildered look on her face.

"Did you see my encounter?" she asks, "I can't remember a thing except it was wonderful."

I knew now why I had felt led to remain on the boat. Through my experience of swimming with the dolphins I had learned that the conscious mind rarely remembers the actual events of an encounter. The feeling remains but the details are gone.

"I saw the whole thing; would you like to know what I saw?"

"Did you really? Would you write it down in my journal?"

My place in her encounter had been a critical one — to observe, to be her memory. I was grateful that I had followed my guidance. The older I grow, the more I listen to that inner "voice."

Day 5, 6:30 AM

Sitting on the upper deck, Suwako and I are greeted by a brilliant sunrise, on this, the last full day of the trip. There are clouds in the sky, though nothing foreboding. The sea is calm and there is no wind.

Suwako leaps from her perch, "Look at the rainbow!" she cries, as the ancient sign of hope adds new color to the morning sky.

"It's a good omen," I reply, just as one of the crew members announces, "It's going to rain; look over there — a squall is heading right for us."

There are always two ways of looking at a situation, I muse. Sometimes if the dolphins come during a minor storm, the play is especially frolicsome.

Later, the first dolphins appear, only three in this group. Rebecca will take Sugako and Jane, two of the less experienced swimmers, in for a little private audience. Many times these swimmers don't get an opportunity for a meaningful encounter; the better swimmers reach the dolphins first, engage their attention, then gradually pull the action away from the boat. This generous group is agreeable to the plan, wanting the joy of the experience to be shared by all. The dolphins, also generous, gently move to Jane and Sugako, swimming beside them for a time. Their mood reflects the calm of the water, and seeming to sense the level of expertise of those swimming, they try no antics or acrobatics.

Rebecca signals that other swimmers may enter the encounter. I decide to wait, as there are still only three dolphins involved. My turn will come later. How lucky to have the luxury of being generous. Would I be so if I had only today?

Later, settled and reading in the lounge, I become drowsy and nod off. The moment I fall into a dreaming sleep, I am awakened by an announcement that the dolphins have come again, accompanied by a little shower. This time there are four, and I'm the first one in. I am granted another intimate encounter and sense recognition from them. The communication with the dolphins is also familiar. Frances and I swim with a mother and her baby, a poignant reminder of our mother-daughter-like relationship. After the encounter of almost twenty minutes, we return to the boat.

"Do you find it difficult to pull up the mental pictures of what just happened in the water?" I ask Frances.

"Isn't it astounding," she replies in her posh Stratford-on-Avon accent. "I just can't remember a thing, and I want so badly to hold onto it."

I ponder her statement. When swimming with the dolphins, we live completely in the joy and bliss of the moment, then it is gone. Might we also live life in this way? If we entered completely into the joy or pain of each moment, how would our lives be different? By experiencing pain fully, in the moment, could we more easily let it go and move to the next? If we carried no guilt or pain into the next moment of joy, would we not be able to live more fully in that joy?

5:00 PM

We are anchored over the "sugar wreck," the sunken hull of a seventy-year-old sugar freighter. The varieties of fish, coral and water plants are abundant and beautiful. I enjoy a leisurely swim in the clear aquamarine sea, knowing this might be my last chance before we dock at West End for the final night of this trip. Through my mask I see a nurse shark, barracudas, a large ray and a myriad of colorful tropical fish. There is a sense of awe as I am granted this glimpse into a world of teeming activity, where the only sound is my own breathing, the beat of my heart and the click of my camera. Few of the photos I take will develop; the fish are too fast and my camera too slow. The compulsion to somehow save the moment, however, always overrides this knowledge.

After forty-five minutes, I return to the boat and participate in one of my favorite trip activities — a sea bath. Standing on the stern diving platform, still in my swimsuit, I soap up with biodegradable suds, dive into the ocean, then return to the deck to rinse the salt water off with a fresh water hose. Wrapping my head in a towel, I stand on the stern as the warm tropical breeze gently air dries my wet body. There is no other *fresh* I have ever experienced that is quite so delicious. Relaxed, I grab a cold drink from the cooler and sit back, fairly sure there will be no more encounters this trip. Skipper Renee says she will take one more circle around and then we'll return to shore.

Almost immediately we pick up four dolphins who stay, and stay and *stay*. There are three female adults and one tiny grey baby. The mother is amazingly trusting, allowing her baby to swim with us as she remains near. After a short time, she and the aunties go off and the baby plays with us alone! The "corps de ballet" is exquisitely choreographed, as periodically the older dolphins return to weave in and out among the swimmers, checking on their charge.

As always, I make my "signature sound" into my mask, the same sound I have used for six years. The dolphins this year seem to recognize it. At the very least, they are extremely interested and return often to investigate. At one point, three come directly into my mask, making their sounds and waiting for me to respond. We carry on a "sonic" conversation, communicating intimately. They also allow me several tummy rubs, though with my full body suit the sensation is somewhat diminished. The encounter is long, leisurely and generous, both on the part of the dolphins and the humans. There is no intrusion into another's encounter as is the case on many trips. The dolphins share themselves with everyone, as if to ensure that each individual has a meaningful experience.

Twice they leave and return, and I stay in the entire time. Everyone is pleasantly exhausted as we get ready for dinner and the closing circle at West End.

Closing Night Circle

The magical dolphin encounter of earlier in the day sets the mood for the final circle — our last human encounter of the trip. We gather on the upper deck under a sparkling starlit sky that appears close enough to touch. Our hearts are incredibly full; our minds ponder how we will share with the others what this trip has meant. How is it possible to put this experience into words?

In broken English, the Japanese struggle to express their feelings. As with most everyone, they recall as most meaningful the *human* relationships. The dolphins had been the catalyst for human contacts which developed to the deepest level. Yoshiro, through an interpreter, marvels at his discovery of the beauty of his daughter as she swam with the dolphins.

David, the father of the English family, speaks for them, "I am forever changed from this experience," he says. "My entire family is as well." He is positive the feelings will carry over when they return home.

"My expectations were so high, I feared I would be disappointed," Frances quietly says. The experience has exceeded even her lofty expectations.

Rebecca observes that this group never complained when the dolphins didn't come; they continued making their fun with each other.

A young Japanese man named Shingo has recently resigned from a lucrative career as a car designer to search for something more meaningful. I don't remember speaking more than two words to him the whole trip. He is quiet, rather somber and speaks almost no English. He wants to tell us of his meditation at the bow of the boat early one morning.

He begins in Japanese, translated by Suwako. He has difficulty expressing himself, even in his own language. Suwako gropes for the English words as three other Japanese join her attempt at translating his powerful experience. Even then, we are struggling to grasp its meaning. As he continues, his face begins to glow with a smile.

His dark eyes flash as he becomes more animated, speaking rapidly and gesturing with his hands. His excitement and awe are so infectious that I understand everything he is saying, yet understand not one word. This is communication of the soul, similar to being with the dolphins. He had experienced, in that meditation on the bow, the essence of life, the oneness of all things. He was singing for us his Psalm of Thanksgiving, and it was magnificent!

Tomorrow we go our separate paths; I know from other dolphin swims that most of us will never meet again. I read a Psalm I wrote for them, thankful again for the opportunity of being here in this place, in this situation. We all join hands. Rebecca offers her prayer of thanksgiving and encourages others to follow. It is truly a holy and sacred moment.

A Psalm for the Human Pod

They come from many places, have many faces,
In this Human Pod
Gathered for a time, with a common bond
Each has a call of a different kind
From the Other Pod.

We have many languages, different cultures,
In this Human Pod.
Yet we speak the same language
As we learn understanding
From the Other Pod.

We each have hurts we carry,
This Human Pod.
Exposing, for a time, a vulnerable soul
To be healed in some way
By the Other Pod.

We each have expectations,
In this Human Pod,

Of what our adventure will bring.
Will the healing gift be given
By the Other Pod?

There is Patience, Kindness, Understanding,
In this Human Pod,
Drawing us closer and closer together
Every day resembling
The Other Pod.

We will go now, our separate ways,
This Human Pod,
Grateful for the wonder of our experience,
Grateful to the presence of a Mystery
In the Dolphin Pod.

Let us remember as we return home,
O Human Pod,
That we must share *our* gifts of healing,
That we share *our* gifts of loving
With All Other Pods.

Dolphinswim 1996 – Week 2, Day 1

What a difference a day makes! The guests this week bring with them an entirely new atmosphere. At dinner last night in Lucayan Market Square I felt the mood shift dramatically.

Sitting here in the boat lounge, I take up my journaling, tuning out the safety talk I've heard seven times in the past six years.

As does every group, this one has a personality of its own. The participants are a bit rowdy, and I sense they are here to party. There is an anticipation of adventure rather then an attitude of awe and wonder. Numerous German and Swiss, speaking little English, converse among themselves rather than attempting communication with the Americans. There are three women, close friends from Minnesota, traveling together. They bubble with high energy and fun, coming here to be away from families, simply to have a good time.

With the intensity of the previous week's experience still lingering, I find myself avoiding new personal attachments. I feel an unaccustomed sense of completeness, and if I were to go home at this moment I would be satisfied. I'll use this week to concentrate on my writing and just play with the dolphins!

1:00 PM

We are just moving out, a rather late start owing to the low tide. Our first scheduled stop is, again, Bottlenose Bay, where new guests will try out new equipment in a new environment. Many are apprehensive but will be assisted by a crew that is both patient and encouraging. I won't go in, as the sea lice have already found every area on my body not covered by my wet suit. I'll wait for dolphins.

Small groups have already begun forming, divided mostly by language barriers. This doesn't seem to be a very homogeneous group, but I've been wrong before.

3:45 PM

We have almost reached the South Bank, and everyone is ready for a dolphin encounter. Though the water and wind are calm — perfect for the dolphins — our late departure has made this unlikely for today. Captain Renee says weather reports predict it will stay this way for two or three days. The wait begins.

It is "afternoon tea time" — a daily tradition with Horace. Small groups converse over steaming styrofoam cups in the lounge below. The guests are still a little standoffish. I can't decide whether they are unfriendly or just having trouble with the language. Perhaps it is my own mood affecting my perception; I feel no need to "bond" this week. There is a sense, too, that something is shifting the focus of these trips. I had two dreams last night of Dolphinswim and the new boat, both dreams leaving a warm and positive feeling as I awoke. There are no concrete plans as yet; it is a time of waiting.

Through the years I have learned that as the Plan you know is not yours is evolving, the crucial component is patience, the patience to get out of the way and listen.

Day 2, 8:30 AM

We're underway again, heading to the North Sand Bank. Small groups form over coffee or tea, waiting as the promise of Liz's pancakes and sausage waft delicious odors through the lounge. People are getting acquainted, slowly beginning to peel away the onion layers of themselves. Still, they are careful not to share too much too soon.

Last night's opening circle was pleasant, but completely different from the previous week's emotional high. As I suspected, these folks are grown-ups, nice grown-ups, but *definitely* grown-ups. There is none of the childlike wonder of last week. This is not a negative; it just *is*.

My cabin mate, Anne, is long-married, a mother and grandmother, happy with her life. She and her buddies are friendly, but I feel no pressure to become part of their fun-seeking festivities. Others also appear to be on the trip for pleasure rather than a deeper experience. This may change as the week progresses and the dolphins weave their spell. There is a beautiful woman from Holland, whom I met the first evening at dinner. She mentioned a near-death experience of ten years before. I had sensed something special about her when we met, a sort of inner tranquility and peace. Funny, it seems that I am given the opportunity to observe something, knowing it to be real, but not given the explanation until later. I learn things best this way. If I first receive the explanation, I tend to anticipate the experience. If the experience comes, I become suspicious I've just created it.

I don't feel great today. I think I'm catching a cold, a first for me on these trips. My throat is sore, so I am gargling salt water. This seems a bit bizarre since we spend half our time swallowing sea water!

1:00 PM

Still no dolphins, at least none who stay. We see them occasionally as they pass by. Four come alongside, but by the time I don my equipment, ready for an encounter, they disappear. Having already met the challenge of tugging on my wet suit, I go for a swim. The water is perfect, and I enjoy the dip although I'm not sure it's worth the sea lice bites wherever I'm not covered. I don't mind quite so much when there are dolphins.

We circle, trying to attract the dolphins. The second day of the trip is almost over, and this group has had no dolphin encounters. Though they don't complain, the atmosphere is strained as they wait, refusing to move into new *human* encounters.

5:05 PM

We had a fleeting encounter with seven dolphins. Those who went in were excited and felt satisfied. At least it gives them hope the dolphins are around. It seems the dolphins are cruising by, observing the people in this group. Perhaps they are looking for the "children" of last week. It's not going to happen; these people continue to be grown-ups. As much as we have made fun of people who try to figure out why the dolphins come to swim or not, Rebecca and I found ourselves doing it. It does seem that the dolphins come, mingle with the group, then leave. Time will tell.

The guests of this trip stay to themselves or divided into language groups. This works well for me, as I continue writing, reading and nursing my cold.

After dessert, Horace gives his first talk, a rerun for me, but he has a new captive audience and they love him. I go to bed early. It's been sort of a blah day, and the bunk beckons me as my cold medication kicks in.

Middle of the night

It is a recurrent theme in my dream world. It has appeared as long as I can remember.

There is a group of girls with whom I have gone to school, sometimes high school, sometimes college. They are shunning me because they know a secret — something I have done in the past, something so horrible that they refuse to tell me what it is. I don't remember the misdeed but feel a guilt that is unbearable. I know that I must learn the truth in order to be forgiven. I beg them to tell me what it is. "Nothing could be worse than what you are doing to me now," I tell them. The fear I feel at unveiling the secret is great. The pain I feel at the ostracizing by my friends is even greater. I finally convince them to tell me. They show me a vision of what I know to be the past.

There is a large lake on which floats a small rowboat. There are two children in the boat, one older than the other. Both children are girls. I am looking at this from a distance, so I cannot see their faces. I feel that the older one is me. Suddenly the boat capsizes, and the two children fall into the water. The older child tries to save the younger, and as the scene zooms to a close-up view, I am holding a dead child in my arms. When I look at the child's face, I see that she has Down's Syndrome. There is a terrible feeling of guilt and that I am somehow to blame. Then, in my lucid mind I say, "But it wasn't my fault," as I awake.

Awake, I feel relieved, as if a great weight has been lifted from my soul. I feel forgiven, not necessarily by someone else, but in some way I have forgiven myself.

I think it is no accident that yesterday I was writing about parents asking why I was so interested in special children. I had answered, "I have no idea." It was an answer to a question I had often asked myself. The dream had the feel of depicting something that had actually happened, something I was reliving. But knowing nothing like this has ever happened in my lifetime leads me to wonder again about what I believe about reincarnation.

Through the years, I have gone back and forth, sometimes believing multiple lifetimes may be the way the soul continues; other times thinking this to be a metaphor for something more complicated which humans can't comprehend. Often it seemed the only way to explain connections that defy explanation. There was, of course, my Christian upbringing that discouraged my even entertaining the idea, and Christian friends who were horrified at the mention of the word. In recent years I have become comfortable with the stance that reincarnation is one way of viewing the continuation of the individual soul on its eternal journey back to its Source. I know for certain that some part of me existed before I came into this life, and that same part will continue to exist when my physical body dies. I am also certain my life has purpose in this body, and the focus is living in that purpose *now*. Anything other than that, in the end, is simply speculation. I can live with the mystery.

Whatever reality the dream depicted, it cleared away a sense of guilt I have carried into many situations in my life, taking blame on myself for somehow having failed someone I loved. This is the gift of the dream; I will no longer do this.

I do wonder who the Down's child was in the dream. She looked very familiar. She had curly blond hair and blue eyes and was about two years old.

Day 3, Sunday, 6:00 PM

The entire day has gone by with no sign of the dolphins. The wind is blustery, the water rough, the skies cloudy; the guests are impatient and irritable. We have not jelled as a group, and the mood is tense. I am not very sociable either, as I write, cough and blow my reddened nose. I do enjoy my talks with Rebecca as we continue to discuss her new venture. We both feel a sense of already having moved to a new place and time in our respective dolphin journeys.

We are making our last runaround for dolphins before heading into calmer waters for the night.

Finally! Dolphins, and lots of them — more than I've seen at one time on either trip this year. There goes the "no-dolphins-on-Sunday" theory out the ole port hole!

They come in waves on waves, first four, then six more, until there are twenty-five or thirty. They come from every side, surfing the swells of the ocean, the bow and stern wakes. The seas are so rough that the crew decides we must swim in small groups. It is difficult counting heads in the high waves. We are told to stay close together in our group.

The first six go in as others watch from the boat. The dolphins' play reflects the wildness of the ocean. They swoosh by like rockets, racing over shoulders, careening around bodies. Music for this choreography would have to be Beethoven's *Ode to Joy* from the *Ninth Symphony*. As the first group excitedly comes back on board, group two, of which I am a part, prepares for its turn. Four have already gone in, as three of us wait on the platform. "Only two more," the crew member shouts over the roar of the motors. I offer to wait. The others have yet to experience a real encounter on this trip. The dolphins will stay around, and my time will come.

The second group returns to the boat, and our group goes into the water. By now, most of the dolphins have left. There are eight or ten staying to play, among them some mothers and babies. They continue to circulate among the swimmers, giving each one a memorable encounter. I have some wonderful body brushes with the dolphins, while making my signature sound and eye contact with them.

Suddenly, everything seems to go into slow motion. I become aware that four dolphins, Rebecca, and I are swimming apart from the other swimmers. The water is still turbulent, but the dolphins are behaving as they would if the water were completely calm. We float, leisurely, in pod formation, barely seeming to move at all. I begin making my sounds, varying them to match the sounds the dolphins make. I express with my sounds the gratitude I am feeling in my heart for this incredible experience. They respond, sometimes imitating me, at other times, creating new sounds. We carry on a multifrequency conversation. There is much tummy rubbing, so feathersoft that in my wet suit I am not sure I am being touched, but they are so close! There is such intimacy in this moment — or is it an hour, or a day? I have no conception of time.

In past years, I have observed from a distance as Rebecca interacts with the dolphins. Her intimate relationship with them is built upon years of encounters and communication. When the dolphins swim with her, she is the center of their attention, as if no one else exists. To be included in the pod with Rebecca and the dolphins is a precious gift. Wide-eyed with wonder, we return to the boat, both feeling the encounter to be a consecration of some kind.

Day 4, 8:30 AM

Very windy day and rough, even though we've come all the way in to Sandy Cove. There is a question as to whether we will venture out to find the dolphins. The wind is from the southeast which means going out would be fine, but coming in would be extremely rough.

9:30 AM

The report from the skipper is that the wind will keep us at Sandy Cove for the day. In groups of five, the inflatable Zodiak takes people to the island. Since I went last week, I decide to stay on the boat to read and write. I might even treat myself to a little sun. I have been very good these two weeks. No one would know that I've been on a boat in the Bahamas. My dermatologist would be proud!

12:30 PM

Had a nice morning, with almost everyone gone to the island. It was quiet, and I got a great exercise workout on the deck with music, then treated myself to a little sun.

People are returning now for a lunch of Mexican food. Soon we will pull the anchor and head out to dolphin territory where it will be so rough we won't be able to swim even if we see dolphins. Everyone has taken mega-doses of Dramamine, which sends them to their bunks or into the lounge for naps. This will be our last trip out to the Banks.

Day 5

This trip sort of fizzled out to a disappointing end, at least for most of this week's guests. They really only had one good encounter during the entire six days. They seemed to take it well, as they know it is the luck of the draw in this world of dolphins. The weather was certainly a factor. Sometimes I feel the dolphins are not showing up to protect us from ourselves; if they are there we would go in no matter what the conditions.

We go into West End a day early and participate in activities offered by this part of Grand Bahama Island. There is swimming and sunning on a lovely beach, snorkeling off shore and time for leisurely walks. Human relationships have been encouraged by the scarcity of dolphins.

I decide to take a walk. Rita, a Swiss-German woman, asks if I would mind if she joins me. The truth is I *do* mind; my walks are always taken alone and are meditative in nature. I normally have no trouble telling someone this and feel no guilt in the process. But for some reason, I can't bring myself to tell her "no." I have spoken to her only briefly during the trip and, if I am honest with myself, have rather avoided her. It is obvious that she is painfully shy and has trouble relating to this rather boisterous crowd. She speaks little English, but we manage to have an intimate discussion about the hurt caused by the Catholic Church in which she grew up. She, like so many others I have met, has become disillusioned and is now involved in metaphysical philosophy and New Age. As I have done in the past with folks like this, I share my personal perspective relating to my Christian faith, bridging the gap with my own knowledge of New Age and how I had assimilated it. There is such a hunger in her to return to the real Truth of what she learned as a child, yet it is extremely difficult to separate this Truth from the dogma that had driven her away. I ask whether she still prays. She replies she no longer feels comfortable praying; she has no idea who God is and only remembers the prayers associated with her negative church experience. She feels abandoned and alone. I promise that I will pray for her and suggest she begin some sort of new search for the faith of her childhood. We part, knowing it is unlikely we will ever see each other again.

Such is the nature of these trips. I always feel the urgency of making the most of every human encounter. Again I was grateful I had followed my guidance. By sharing an expression of love and compassion, I may have made a difference in her life. It is for this, after all, that humans are drawn here; it is this we receive from the dolphins. The unconditional acceptance and love we feel in their presence, aliens in *their* world, is a reminder that we, too, must offer these expressions in every *human* encounter. For in truth, we make aliens of ourselves when we separate from each other by race, religion, nationality, or other differences we choose to divide ourselves.

The Narrow Gate

There are so many who don't believe
In a God of any kind.
In disappointment and disillusionment they cry,
How could a God allow this to happen?
How could a merciful God allow
Children to starve
Disease to kill
Hate to increase?
In the name of God
Genocide has eliminated races.
Holy wars have raged.
Money has been taken from the poor.
Does this say something about God?
Or does it tell us about ourselves?

When we, the believers, define God too narrowly
Are we closing the gate?
The invitation to "ask, seek, knock, enter"
Is open to all.
These are first steps.
They are steps of faith.
If we who already believe
Wish to show others the Way
We must not close the Gate by
Judgment, Exclusion, Self-Righteousness, Prejudice.
This is the "wide gate," the "easy road."
The narrow gate of faith, the road that is "hard"
Is opened by
Forgiveness, Inclusion, Humility, Love.
We must define God by the way we treat others.
If we define Him by dogma only
We close the Gate.
Lord, let us who believe
Become Gatekeepers
Who always assure
That the Gate remains open.

Day 6

Because of our anti-climatic last day, we decide to forego the closing circle. Everyone drifts off into small groups, some going into town to party at a bar. It is a strange ending for a strange week.

1:30 PM

As I fly home, rereading my journal notes, I realize that for the first time I have a vivid memory of a dolphin encounter, and an intense feeling of wonder and mystery remain. My mind returns again and again to the encounter two days before with Rebecca and the dolphins. The sharp, clear mental images, the symphony of sounds, the depth of my emotions are indelibly imprinted on my mind, my heart, my soul. If it were to be the last dolphin encounter I ever had, it would have been more than I could ever have hoped.

It was a Sacrament.

It was a Benedictus.

The Word

Out of the Chaos, we can recreate the World.
Out of the Ashes, our Phoenix can rise.
Out of the Sorrow, we can bring joy again.
Out of the Hate ... Love's surprise.

In the beginning, before the Word,
There was no order in the Formless Void,
No Meaning, only Power.
Then a Mighty Wind,
Swept over the Dark Abyss,
And out of the Chaos ... A Flower.

Now cities are burning, with the fires of Rage,
Leaving us to ask ourselves,
"What went wrong?"
Then the Sound of Voices
Join together in Harmony,
And out of the Ashes ... A Song.

A Mother gazes at her Starving Child,
So painful that we look away,
We turn our head.
Then looking back, Compassion wins,
We do our Part,
And out of the Sorrow ... Bread.

We judge another's Soul according to our point of view,
We chart another's Course
By the Color of his Face,
Then finally we realize
That All are One,
And out of the subtle Hate ... Grace.

Out of the Chaos, we will Co-create the World.
Our Phoenix flies and becomes a Dove.
Hate and Sorrow changed
By the blowing of a Gentle Wind.
And there's only one Word,
And the Word is Love.

XIII
Reprise

September, 1996

Something is missing! Since the Dolphinswim trip in May, I have been compiling my journal notes and a box full of related materials from the past twenty-eight years into some semblance of order. Though the story is coming together well, telling it in the first person is cumbersome and uninteresting. It is time for one of my walks.

I take my usual route out to Boonsboro Road. So many memories are associated with this familiar trek.

There have been walks for exercise, for relaxation, for inspiration and prayer.

There was one walk filled with terror, followed by walks plagued by fear.

There were exuberant walks filled with joy, meditative walks pondering losses.

I pass the spot where I recommitted to my marriage as it went through a difficult period.

I pass a flowering shrub that on one spring day released the pungent perfume reminding me of my beloved grandmother.

I trudge up the hill where one snowy morning I relived childhood memories of sledding, open fires and hot cocoa with marshmallows.

All in all, these three miles mark an incredible and wonderful journey lasting almost twenty-eight years.

This particular walk is an "in-search-of" kind of walk. I need help. The story I have lived is a good one, an unusual one; yet I feel it would be more powerful if told, at least in part, from a perspective other than my own. I prayerfully pose the question, "Who might have known me from the beginning of my story? Who would have been present at each event I describe?"

At the very moment I pass the greying wooden fence nearing the Stop sign, I suddenly become aware of a presence that I can only describe as completely filling me.

"I have been here all along. I know more about your story than you know yourself."

I recognize the presence instantly as a flood of awareness washes over me. It is Robin Elizabeth, the little girl with Down's Syndrome whose story had inspired my passion for helping special children. There is also a revelation in this moment that this "angel unaware" had, indeed, been with me all along. The implications of this revelation are infinite and fill me with wonderment. If she had been there, what must she know?

She finally knows about me! What a blessing! Even though time is supposed to mean nothing here, it felt like forever before I was allowed to let her know of my presence in her life.

Now, with my help, she is putting together the pieces of her life's puzzle. Her confidence is a bit shaken after so many publishers rejected her psalms. Does she really have a story that would be of interest to anyone besides herself? Will the pieces of her puzzle at last come together in a way that has meaning? Will the whole picture appear?

And oh, what a puzzle it is — what a journey! Libby Layne must sort through countless odd pieces of various shapes, sizes and colors. Throughout the journey she experienced great joy and excitement when sections of the puzzle picture took form. Often she faced disappointment and frustration when a seemingly perfect piece wouldn't fit or became lost.

From each trial working the puzzle, however, she learned lessons which led her forward. Her journey illustrates that for those who choose to be aware, life is a series of connected events which ultimately fit together in a beautiful picture.

To sustain her on this adventure she received three wonderful gifts: the gift of love of and talent for music, the gift of compassion for special children like me, and most importantly, the gift of a "spirit of tenacity." It is this gift which urges her forward, giving her determination to find meaning in every experience. It is through this gift that "we" guide and help her to learn her life's lessons. We encourage her awareness.

She carries into her future two lessons in particular which she has learned in her journey so far.

The first is this: There is no box top with a picture of the finished puzzle, because the puzzle never stops changing form; the puzzle is never finished.

The second: It is working the puzzle that gives the journey meaning, not completing it.

The journey is never over; the Journey *is the* Puzzle.

I know what you're thinking: "But she hasn't solved the mystery of the Sound of the Dolphin's Psalm yet! You can't just end a book about a mystery and not solve it. It's just not done!"

Where better to solve the mystery of a sea mammal than at the sea, particularly the sea in which she had her first dolphin encounter?

Libby Layne is going to Virginia Beach for a weekend and is taking with her the tapes of her DOLFA-WAVE study. She has requested my help in reviewing them, knowing now that I am part of her story. She is hoping I will give her the answer to the mystery as we watch them together. I will do only what I have done in the past — I will guide her to her own awareness.

Virginia Beach, June 1996

I begin watching the tapes filmed almost two years ago during the DOLFA-WAVE study. They record every moment of the sessions in the Dolphin Room for that month in October. After the disappointing response from my experts, I filed them away and have not watched them since.

The mounted video camera I used was turned on immediately before the child entered the Dolphin Room and turned off when the child went out the door. Because the camera was stationary, certain areas of the room were out of range. Every sound was recorded, however, and along with the notes I took, the tapes document well what happened there.

The first meeting was an orientation, using no dolphin sounds. This gave me an opportunity to observe the child's reaction to the room itself and develop ideas for activities I might use in the sessions. Parents and sometimes siblings were present. For the next month, twice a week, I spent twenty minutes with the child as the dolphin sounds were played through two speakers. As soon as the child and parent felt comfortable, I was left alone with him or her. I let each child set the pace and tone of the sessions, improvising as I went along.

Dylan:

During the entire orientation, Dylan lies on the floor in a passive, lethargic daze. His mother and I discuss the procedure of future sessions and how to fill out forms, targeting specific behaviors to be observed. He ignores me, paying no attention to the room or its contents.

During the next four sessions, I observe and take notes as Dylan and his mother participate in the imitative method used in his room at home.

Each time I begin playing the dolphin sounds, he places himself near a speaker or in between them. He sometimes takes a sitting position; at other times, he lies down, curled up in a fetal position, sucking his thumb.

In one session he becomes very affectionate with his mom, sitting in her lap. As she talks softly to him, he makes intense eye contact. Both of these things are noted by her to be very unusual. It appears there are times when he listens to the sounds, and at these times there is no self-stim or "isms" as his mother calls them.

I enter the "play" but am not acknowledged as being there. There are times when he makes eye contact with me across the room, and I say, "Hello Dylan, I see you looking at me." There is nothing quite as powerful as eye contact with an autistic child. It is a rare privilege granted only at *their* discretion. The only thing that rivals it, giving me the same feeling, is looking into the eye of a dolphin.

At session five, mother leaves me alone with Dylan. When he decides to sit or lie down, again he chooses to be near the speakers. Pacing around the room, he frequently goes to the door, turning the knob around and around. This is another of Dylan's "isms," behaviors which he ritually performs. He takes my hand, leading me around the room. When I present a bag of toys, he looks into it. I have captured his attention for a moment.

As he allows me into his world, acknowledging my presence, I speak to him softly and gently stroke his back. He is responding to my touch and relaxes. When I try placing him on my lap as his mother had done in a former session, he resists and cannot get comfortable. I am rushing things, getting too close too soon. When he appears to listen to the dolphin sounds, he is completely still and there is no self-stim. This usually happens when the dolphin communication is more animated and "chatty," as in the sequence with the mother and baby dolphin.

When I sing *Oom-Pa-Pa,* I hear his first vocalization. It is similar to a baby's coo, and when he makes it, there is eye contact.

During session six, Dylan and I exchange imitations as he had with his mother. His "isms" include rubbing the rug or pounding three or four times on the floor, then waiting for a response from the other person. He will spin any object given him, which today is a small pillow. He becomes interested in the toys in the bag, and when I begin voicing a cat hand puppet, he responds to it with his own sounds. He makes "uh" and "ah" and other cooing sounds, looking directly at the puppet. *He is communicating.* He becomes calm and attentive when the "chatty section" of the dolphin communication comes on. At the end of the session, I say, "Do you want to see your mama?" To this he responds with a vocalization while going to the door.

The next session shows Dylan in front of the other speaker, placed across the room. We have long eye contact, vocalizations and no self-stim during his stay there. He is not interested in the bag of toys today. During the session, Dylan ruminates constantly, regurgitating food up into his mouth, then chewing it. This is another of his "isms" and is particularly messy today because of coughing spells. During the times he is engaged in listening, vocalizing to the puppet, or paying attention to me, he stops ruminating. He follows me with his eyes if I go to the camera or anywhere in the room. During the mother/infant dolphin sequence, he lies in front of the speaker, completely still with no self-stim or ruminating. He responds to it with a vocalization. As soon as the next section begins, during which there are fewer dolphin sounds, he begins ruminating again.

At the last session in the Dolphin Room, Dylan enters the room very animated and begins an excited floor pounding which he expects me to imitate. When we finish this game, he reaches out with his hand and gently rubs my face while making a vocalization. He continues to calm down, and his self-stim lessens. He smiles, makes eye contact, touches my face, and makes vocalizations. He even devises a game in which he lowers his head to the floor, looks up at me, then waits for me to imitate. Throughout the session he is very aware and curious. He goes about the room observing its contents, feeling certain objects and making "comments." Consistent with other sessions, during the mother/infant sequence, he lies still, attentive to the sounds, smiling to himself.

When the sounds go off at the end of the session, he sits up in a very "regular kid" sort of position and his expression is not at all blank but "in this world." He makes eye contact with me and is completely calm but not tuned out. He then goes over to the lights on the sound system and makes a high squealing noise of pleasure as he looks at them.

As I watch the tapes, I relive the feeling associated with each event. After checking my notes, I find I don't see any more or any less than I did two years ago. I wonder, Robin, am I seeing only what I want to see? Am I so positive that something in that room makes a difference that I am blind to the truth? I have given up the need to prove anything scientifically, yet I feel there is something important happening there. Do you have any comments, Robin?

"Not really, Libby Layne. What you see, you see. What you feel, you feel. It is unimportant whether anyone else sees or feels it. This mystery of The Sound of the Dolphin's Psalm is still unfolding. Keep watching the tapes, keep learning. Trust yourself and your journey.

Kim:

Alike in many ways, Kim and Dylan have no verbal communication and have had a life of seizure activity. So the question is, as always, has there been extensive brain damage, or is there some understanding, merely blocked by autistic behaviors? Kim's mother is certain there is intelligence behind Kim's tightly closed mouth and defensive body position. Would the safety of the Dolphin Room release some of her inhibitions and allow us into her world or would she venture into ours?

During the orientation session with her mother present, Kim assumes what I would come to know as her protective position, mouth contorted in a pinched grimace, arms bent at the elbows, hands near her face, clinched tightly. With stiff legs she walks about the room. When she stops, she places one foot in front of the other and rocks back and forth in a repetitive self-stim movement. She appears nervous and uncomfortable.

Continuing the mode of communication I used when I met her at her home, I speak to her as an adult who understands everything I say. She is not responsive to me. As I explain the forms and procedure to her mother, Kim stops her pacing intermittently, appearing to attend our conversation. I direct my attention to Kim, telling her again what will be happening in the room. She makes no eye contact, and I see no response to what I am saying. I ask if she wants to hear some music and suggest that she point to the sound system if she does. She responds by pointing to it. The music plays quietly and seems to calm her as I allow her space and time to adjust. On the way out the door, her mother says, "Give Libby a high five." She turns to me, instead, reaching out for a hug.

For the next three sessions Kim is accompanied by either her mother, her aide Stacie, or both. Before the dolphin sounds are turned on, Kim is locked into her tight protective position. As the sounds begin, Stacie encourages her to sit on the floor.

She now assumes a position her mother has never seen before. Her arms unwind and relax as she lowers herself to the floor. She then pulls her legs up into a fetal position hugging her knees with her arms. She appears relaxed and comfortable. There is some rocking and arm-waving self-stim occasionally, but at times she is completely still and appears to be listening to the dolphin sounds.

Pulling her ear and twisting her hair are two signals Kim's mother believes indicate that she is listening. As the dolphin sounds continue, she does both. She relaxes and begins to smile. We ask her to pull her ear if the sounds are bothering her. At a particular section, she pulls her ear. She does this several times when the sounds are either of a very high frequency or intense. Is this just a coincidence?

When the "chatty" mother/infant sequence begins, she smiles and looks at the speaker. I tell her this is a mother and a baby dolphin communicating, then jokingly say, "You probably know what they are saying!" She smiles broadly, and her body language indicates she perceives the humor of my comment.

The next two sessions are less interactive, as she becomes unresponsive and defiant. Either her mom or Stacie are always present and are unsuccessful at getting her to cooperate. She pays no attention to me at all. At the end of the third session I am visibly frustrated as I ask her why she is behaving in this way. She responds by roughly pushing me away with her hands.

When Kim returns for the next session, her mother and I ask if she would be comfortable meeting alone with me. She is, after all, a grown woman of twenty-eight. If we are to treat her as such, perhaps she would respond better to me without her mother present. She doesn't answer but does not object. Her mother leaves the room, and I am left with Kim.

Ill at ease, she is still not relating to me, avoiding my gaze and walking away from any conversation I attempt with her. She refuses to sit down, and I begin wondering if this was a good idea after all.

I try another approach. I apologize for my frustration with her in the previous session, explaining I just didn't understand. "I am very sorry," I say. She immediately looks me in the eye, relaxes and reaches out to give me a hug! Did she understand my words or only my intention? It really doesn't make any difference; we have *communicated.*

For the remainder of the sessions, I proceed on the premise that Kim does, indeed, understand everything I say and that she is also intelligent enough to comprehend more advanced communication.

I ask her mother if Kim has ever heard the word "autism" or had any previous knowledge of this as part of her problem. She answers, "No, I've never told her anything like that." I receive permission to introduce her to the books written by Donna Williams, an autistic woman who had battled to overcome some of her autistic behaviors. Donna is the same age as Kim and in her books gives a remarkable account of how it feels to live in an autistic person's world.

From this intelligent woman's testimony, professionals are learning first hand what it means to be autistic. If Kim relates to Donna, might an understanding of her disability help her overcome it? It is a long shot, but Kim's mother agrees it is worth a try.

In my first full session alone with Kim, I begin telling her of the disorder, autism. My explanation includes information I would give anyone to whom autism is an unknown — facts about behaviors, history, and the frustrations that accompany it. I suggest the possibility that she is autistic. Her attention and eye contact are intense, and there are many times when she twists her hair or gives me some sign that indicates she understands or is at least listening. She is intent as I read passages from Donna's book in which she expresses how it feels to be autistic. I choose sections that might apply to Kim and find that she responds particularly to Donna's poetry.

At one session, I read portions of Kim's Facilitated Communication dialogues and encourage her to "get angry" at some of the things which she "said" made her angry. I suggest she might scream or throw pillows. This frightens her, so I don't pursue it. We also approach the subject of her reason for not talking, which she discusses in FC. The only response I get is an intense eye contact.

Throughout the two weeks, there are times when she withdraws completely or goes back to her self-stim movements. She will sometimes point to Donna's book as a signal that I read. During passages that express great pain and poignant descriptions of frustrations experienced by Donna, eye contact is intense, and I feel that she too is expressing pain.

She allows me to touch her only lightly, and if I get too close she moves away. I work to help her relax her standing body position which is still rigid and protective. She tries but it is extremely difficult for her. She always assumes her "listening" position, with knees tucked when she sits down. Sometimes we sit silently; sometimes I sing or talk. After the two weeks of the sessions are concluded, I feel she has allowed me into her world for at least moments at a time.

Did Kim understand a word I said or were all her reactions merely movements of a brain-damaged individual who had no idea that anything unusual was going on? That was what one of my "experts" said. She saw no reaction, no response, no smiles, no understanding; she saw nothing but a woman whose seizures had left her hopelessly retarded. Robin, are her mother and I just dreamers who want there to be a person inside that tightly strung body?

Remember the lesson of Pringle, Libby Layne — how they said at the Training Center he was a "Big O"? By this they meant there was no hope. There are those, like you, who see past the exterior shell, who can reach the soul and spirit inside it. On some level, Kim did understand every word you said. Your explanations and your reading of Donna's book reached her at that level of understanding. Whether it is the way you understand or not, your choosing this way of communicating worked for her.

It was the same situation with Pringle years ago. When you heard his pitiful weeping and wailing many times, you wondered if he felt abandoned. One day you explained, as if he understood perfectly, how hard it must have been for his mother to leave him at the Training School. You assured him that she loved him very much. After that, he cried, but there was never again that terrible wailing he had done for so long. Though he may not have understood the words themselves, he understood your loving him enough to communicate with him in this way.

You must understand that communicating as we do here is also very unique. We don't speak with words as you do, but with thoughts, born on the wings of love. Here, the power of love has no bounds. Anyone can appreciate this kind of communication, no matter what their disability. For Pringle, Dylan and Kim, whose language is so limited, this is the only language they can comprehend. Think also about your communication with the dolphins!

There is something I've been waiting a long time to tell you, something about your time with Pringle. I had to wait until you knew I was a part of your story. You need to know the meaning of one very special day.

It is Memorial Day. Do you remember that day, Libby Layne? It is a beautiful spring morning, a holiday. You decide that since there will be only a few staff members there and no special things like Hadley's music class, or the blind program, you will go see Pringle. You have worked with him now for almost nine months, and he is eleven years old.

Several days before, you had the dream about Pringle being healed. He was talking and singing and teasing you with his eyes. This dream is probably on your mind as you go to the Training School and take Pringle outside for a walk. You decide not to do any music, just spend time with him sharing the beautiful day.

Remember when you go under the tree, how he looks up at the leaves as if he really is seeing them? You quietly say, "That's a tree, Pringle," and he keeps looking and looking. He is not rocking back and forth, chewing his shirt or gazing into space. You become aware he is aware of everything around him. His movements are very smooth, not jerking as is usual. He is looking all around now, at the trees, the sky, the ground, and then, suddenly he looks AT you — not THROUGH you or AROUND you, but right at your eyes — and makes eye contact. Do you remember how you felt when he looked at you? It was the same feeling and look as in your dream.

He then begins to look very closely at the bright blue arm of his wheelchair and strokes it with his hand. You are certain he is exploring it for the first time. His concentration is complete, but not like when he gets fixed on his bells or other objects. He looks at his fingers, just like a little baby, moving them back and forth in the sunlight. He smiles and giggles with delight, and you watch, spellbound.

Time does one of those funny things when you don't know how long it has been, and after a while, you take him back to the porch. You bring out a large mirror. When you put the mirror in front of him, he does what all children do the first time they see themselves. He laughs, reaches out, and pulling the mirror to himself, kisses his image! He has seen mirrors before, all over the day hall and in the therapy rooms, but he has never done this. He makes sounds to the image in the mirror, sometimes going back to some of his self-stim movements. It's as if seeing himself is too powerful, and he must go back inside himself to handle it.

After you take away the mirror, you do something you've done many times before; you try to get him to grab his nose or your nose, saying, "Where's Pringle's nose, where's Libby's nose?" He has never paid any attention to this before. Today, he reaches out, grabs your nose and holds. You begin talking in a funny voice that happens when you hold your nose. Pringle giggles and laughs, then explores your face like a blind person. He gently touches your cheeks, your eyes, your mouth, smiling and looking. He then strokes your hair like you do to him all the time and lets you know he wants to hug. Today he really hangs on, not his usual quick, fleeting hug.

During all of this Pringle is in "this world" completely, and you don't want to breathe for fear you'll break the spell. It's exactly the same feeling as in your dream. It's as if Pringle has a great secret and has been fooling everyone all along. You are excited and positive this will be a new beginning for Pringle. You can almost see him going home and can't wait for his family to see him like he is today. It's the miracle of the dream come true!

But it never happens again, you know — not the way it had that day. There are little windows of time when you see the Pringle of Memorial Day, but only glimmers. You keep trying for five years after that to bring back the Pringle you met that day.

Don't you see what Pringle did? Don't you realize that if he hadn't shown you who he really was inside, you might not have stayed to learn your lessons with him? He "came out" that day just for you to see that inside, in the place where he really lives, there is peace. Even though on the outside he is crippled, mentally retarded, blind, and living in a place that seems less than a home, on the inside, in the world to which he has returned, he is at peace. For a time, he will remain on the earth, until his mission is finished and he teaches all the lessons he agreed to teach. He will then, as I did, break the bonds of the battered shell that is his earthly body and be free.

Keep this in mind as you think about your time with Kim and Dylan. There is more to communication than words.

You're wondering about the dolphin sounds aren't you? How do they fit into the picture? Continue watching the tapes and listening to your spirit; the Truth is there, you only must become aware of it.

James:

James comes in like a whirlwind, accompanied by his mother and sister for his orientation session. He is in constant motion. Unlike Dylan and Kim, James is verbal, and though his vocabulary is minimal, he uses it appropriately and can articulate up to three- or four-word sentences. He is very rough with his mother and sister, and it is evident that this is normal interaction between them. His mother constantly reprimands him, with little success. As in the home visit, he does not acknowledge my presence. At one time he backs up to me, watching the action in the mirror. As he leaves, he has a tantrum and is non-compliant. It will be interesting to note any changes when the sounds begin next session.

Again at the next full session, James's mother and his sister, Maria, are present. The dolphin sounds begin. James is noisy, active, and jumping all over his mom. He plays with toys he has brought, noisily but appropriately building a road with Legos and playing with a car. He loves the mirrors, making faces and gyrating with his body in front of them. Several times as the dolphin sounds become conversational, he appears to listen, but there is no visible response. He squeals in a high-pitched voice and is hyperactive. Since his mother has told me of his hyper-hearing, it is noteworthy that the sounds do not appear to bother him.

As his mother says, "Listen!" James goes to the speaker with his toy stethoscope, puts the end up to it, and listens intently to the sounds. He begins treating the speaker "like a person" with his doctor kit. He smiles and concentrates intently on his play. Going to the other speaker, he repeats putting his ear up to the speaker, then the stethoscope. He tries to determine how the sounds are being made by following the cord from the speaker. It is obvious that James is very intelligent and understands abstract concepts. After a time, he loses interest and goes back to playing with Maria. He is now much calmer. He crawls into a box and assumes a fetal position, where he stays for a time. As he "tunes out" the sounds, he becomes hyperactive again and becomes aggressive to Maria. She is also fairly active, and I am anxious to see how James will respond when she is not present.

In session two, James, for the first time, acknowledges my presence in his world. I had put a real, but unhooked, phone in the room. He immediately begins looking for a hookup outlet. This is an extremely intelligent little boy. He plays "phone" with me as his mother watches. After about four minutes, he becomes aware of the dolphin sounds and investigates the sound equipment. He puts his ear to the speaker again and goes to the corner where the amplifier and CD player are. He becomes noncompliant when we ask him to "not touch." He begins imitating the dolphin sounds. His mother says that as a baby, he used to use animal sounds to communicate.

Today there is very little rough housing as he plays with the toys in my bag quietly and appropriately. He and his mother draw with crayons and paper as James verbalizes along with their play. He is not interested in listening to the sounds with the stethoscope as last time, but plays doctor with his mom. Showing that he has a sense of humor, he says, "What's up Doc?" At the end of the session, he becomes very affectionate with his mom.

In session three, James comes into the room hyperactive but immediately calms down and plays with the bag of toys. He accepts me for a short time into the play with his mother. He becomes very interested in a stuffed toy dog with a zip-off coat. His mother notes that he never plays with soft things. He talks *to* and *for* the dog as his mother and I converse. He does not acknowledge the dolphin sounds but is calm and attentive throughout the entire session. He lies down on the floor at one point and plays quietly with the dog.

He engages me in drawing on a large pad with crayons and wants to "trace" the dog's shape. He is completely focused on the task and accepting of me. His mother joins us, and he continues the tracing game as I withdraw. The play is punctuated with dialogue between them. He tells her what he wants her to draw, where and with which color. This continues for ten minutes, at which time his mother smiles and exclaims, "It's incredible — I've never heard him so verbal. I can't believe his language."

James begins the fourth session by immediately going to the toy bag to look for the stuffed dog. He takes it to the pad of paper where he wants to replay the tracing game. Today, I am again invisible to him. He plays for a while, here and there, alone and with his mother. He is calm but does not acknowledge that he is listening to the dolphin sounds. His mother tries coaxing him to the speakers with the stethoscope, but he is not interested. Minutes later, he goes on his own to the speaker, puts his ear to it, and stays in that position for four minutes. He then places his hand on the speaker, and when there is silence between segments, he says, "All gone."

His mother joins him, listening with the stethoscope. He puts it in her ears, then places the other end on the speaker. She comments, and he giggles with delight. When he puts his hand on the speaker and feels the vibration, he exclaims excitedly, "All right!"

He takes the cord from the speaker and puts his ear to it, trying to hear the sounds there. His mother has told him that's where the sound comes into the speakers. This sequence all takes place during the "chatty" mother/calf section. It is obvious James understands every word being said, as his mother comments about how well he is staying in the room and that he must like it. He immediately gets up and goes out the door. This child is a real challenge!

After his mother brings him back into the room, we continue the session. As the sounds quiet down, his hyperactive behavior returns. He ends the session, determined to take home the toy dog to which he has become attached. He runs in circles, clutching the dog, as his mother tries to retrieve it. He finally flings it back over his shoulder, as out the door he goes.

In session five, James acknowledges me immediately as, coming in the door, he gives me a small bag of cereal. His mom says he has been aggressive all weekend. She notes that he is more compliant during the session than anywhere else, though it doesn't seem to carry over afterward. I have noticed in the past that his mother has a tendency to intensify the play, which "revs" James even more. She allows his rough play, even as she tells him no. Several times during today's session I suggest she withdraw when he gets rough. Talking quietly to him and maintaining a relaxed attitude result in his being more calm and compliant. He pays attention to the dolphin sounds only at his mother's suggestion today. At one time he uses a new word added to his vocabulary. Leaning against the speaker, with a smile he remarks, "Cool!"

He also places the stuffed dog's ear on the speaker to listen to the sounds. He is obviously quite taken with the dolphin sounds, and it is a treat having someone able to give me positive feedback that is verbal.

I want to see if Maria's presence will make a difference, now that James seems to be calming down in the sessions. I ask his mother to bring her. There is no doubt that something has changed. Throughout the entire session, James is calm, sometimes playing with me, or Maria, or his mom. He is active, but not rough or aggressive. The only time he becomes a bit hyperactive is when his mother tries to get him to attend to her. James and I have a long session in which he involves me with a bandana in play. He makes me "disappear," and we put the bandana on the dog. There is generous eye contact. It seems to be difficult for his mother to remain out of the "action" for long, and she joins us. Comparing the first two sessions in which Maria was present with this one, it is apparent that something in the room helps James to calm down.

Due to circumstances at James's home, it has been almost two weeks since our last session. When James comes in with Maria and his mom, he immediately sits down with me to play. I am so intrigued with this that I begin play without turning on the dolphin sounds. James is quiet, calm and attentive. His mother reminds me that the dolphin sounds have not been turned on. James follows me with his eyes as I go to the amplifier and push the CD button. I return and sit down with him. For some reason, the sounds still don't start, so I go again to the equipment as he waits patiently for me. The sounds finally begin.

For almost half the session we play with a puzzle, the puppet and the dog. At one time he stops everything and listens to the sounds intently. When I begin talking with his mom, he taps my leg to draw back my attention.

He becomes distracted and agitated. He and Maria "mug" in front of the video camera. When it is time to stop, he balks at the "no," kicking and hitting me. Mother intercedes, calming him down as he quickly gets focused on the toys in the bag. It is highly unusual for him to give up his tantrum this easily. He brings me into the play again and lies down near me and lets me rub his back. It seems almost an apology. He is very quiet and focused. Again, even with Maria there, he has had a good session. I really wish I could have him alone. Last time it was agreed we would try, but it seems the mother has reconsidered. She did not mention it and neither did I, as I don't want to prolong the study any longer. I have already finished with everyone else.

On November 5, James's mother calls. Even though the study sessions are finished, she wants him to have another session; she says that after a very bad morning, during which James has "lost it" twice, he needed to come.

He comes in like a tornado, obviously out of control already. He runs to the next room where he picks up a plastic ball and bat. He has a tantrum as we try to take it away. He even throws the stuffed dog angrily. This behavior goes on for about eight minutes, during which the dolphin sounds are turned up in volume. He finally lies down on the floor with a plastic toy which he rattles in a self-stim type movement, calming himself down. He still won't engage in play but fiddles around with the dog, puzzles and other toys, as if trying to figure out what he'll do next. After a time, he begins a game with me of the previous session — putting puzzle pieces in the cat puppet's mouth. He makes no eye contact, but is physically very close and is calm and quiet. Eventually he lays his head gingerly on my knee. I speak to him in hushed tones. His mother raises the noise level with her voice. I suggest a more quiet approach, to which she responds, as does James. She begins tickling him; again I suggest she keep it calm. James remains calm, listening to the sounds and holding the puppet up to his face. His hand is placed near me, and he allows me to take it. He makes intense eye contact with me for several moments, then breaks it off when it's too much for him. As the sounds end, he goes over to the camera and gets up on the table. With a little coaxing, he comes down, with no return to the behavior of the beginning of the session. There is no question at all that the experience of the Dolphin Room is a positive one for him. I only wish his mother would allow me to continue working with him alone.

You don't even need to ask me on this one do you, Libby Layne? It's right there on the tape. You do realize that you needn't worry about what the "expert" said — that she saw no change at all. Perhaps she didn't watch the whole thing, or perhaps she just didn't know what you were looking for.

There is an important point you may have missed in one of James's sessions. He came into the room and was immediately calm, even before you turned on the dolphin sounds.

The dolphin sounds have something to do with the mystery, but they are only a part of the whole picture. I want you to watch yourself with these children, how you relate to them. Watch how they react to you, your love and acceptance of them. The surroundings you created make a difference, too — the colors, the calm mood of the room, and the healing energy that abides there.

Before you began, your minister performed a "blessing" ceremony in the Dolphin Room and dedicated it to a healing ministry. That was not only a formality or ritual, but a sacrament. It created a sacred space, a holy place where you would do what you are doing.

Isn't it odd? The many variables which you worried would prevent a scientific study are now the very things working together to produce the results you see. More variables exist than you are even aware of. You needn't be aware of them to know something special is happening there. And don't forget, we were there too, helping you along.

Patrick:

Enter Patrick, curious about everything in the room. He immediately goes to the camera and puts his eye up to it. He is as tall as I and weighs more. His round, pleasant face looks to be much younger than his eleven-year-old body, and his actions are more like those of a five-year-old. He reminds me of a St. Bernard puppy, bounding around the room. He opens and shuts the doors of cabinets. He moves to the mirrors, takes various body positions and makes funny faces. When he discovers the speakers, I tell him that is where the dolphin sounds will come out.

"Where are the dolphins?" he asks.

I can see that this will be a whole new set of challenges as I try to explain the workings of the sound system. Patrick is not only verbal but obviously quite intelligent and interested in the world around him.

With him are his mother and teenage sister. The mother encourages Patrick's silly behaviors in her strident school teacher voice. She tries to draw his sister into the antics, but she is reticent and obviously embarrassed. Here is a typical teenage girl who must not only contend with a younger brother, but one who has strange, inappropriate behaviors. I am reminded of the many adjustments a family with an autistic child must make.

As his mother and I begin to talk about the study and parent forms, Patrick "tunes out." He shakes the crayon box, taps and flips the drawing board, and makes various other noises which are meant either to draw our attention back to him or phase us out of his world.

He walks over to me and says, "O.K. Libby, time to go home."

I am pleased that he has remembered my name, added to the fact that he is the first of my subjects who is able to verbalize it.

Patrick is very active, constantly trying to involve his sister in his silliness at the mirrors. He vacillates between appropriate conversation with an impressive vocabulary and nonsense talk in answer to questions. His sentences are stilted and usually composed of four or five words. Two of his favorite phrases that are a staple in his conversations are "all to pieces" and "falling apart." Many of his nonsense sentences are probably from cartoons and other TV programs that he watches. They are used as fill-ins for silence or for tuning out mechanisms when there is too much confusion around him. There are times when he appears to understand every word, yet can't communicate. He then resorts to his pat phrases. Another favorite is "chicken."

He becomes interested in my drawing *for* him. His mother says this is how one of his teachers first began getting him to talk again at eight years of age. He would tell her what to draw, and they would discuss the picture. He knows what he wants drawn and knows his colors well enough to ask for specific ones for specific things.

As we draw, I become aware of the extent, not only of his grasp of language and vocabulary, but of his sensitivity. Patrick is a poet! At his request, we are drawing his sister. He tells me to draw her earrings.

"What color are they, Patrick?"

"Golden."

"What color are her eyes?"

"They are blue like the sky, like the stars."

Then, teasing her he says, "She has a big nose, big ears."

When we all laugh, he goes back to nonsense sentences, "Her face is shattered all to pieces."

As I draw her face he says, "Make an expression."

Back and forth we go, from an intelligent normal conversation to a confused set of nonsensical phrases.

What a strange disorder. What a mystery!

As he leaves, he gives me a "high five" and says, "See you later, alligator."

This is going to be fun!

On Tuesdays, because his mother teaches, I must pick Patrick up at his school. This is one of those variables that will make a purely scientific approach impossible.

Today Patrick is confused and ill at ease. Individuals with autism don't like variation in their routine, even if it is something they will enjoy. Order in their world means that we do the same thing, at the same time in the same way. No surprises. Maintaining this order is of utmost importance.

Patrick remembers me, and as we ride over to the Dolphin Room, I explain why he left school and what we will be doing. When we reach the room, he seems to be more at ease and remembers the orientation session of the previous Saturday.

As he is finishing his lunch, I look over his school work, impressed with his math and reading skills. One of his exercises at school that day was to describe the contents of a room. After turning on the dolphin sounds, I ask him to tell me the contents of the room, "What's in this room, Patrick?"

"Dolphin sounds."

He is not actively listening to the sounds, but as with the other children, he is not at all bothered by them.

He explores the room, going to the speakers and listening to each one for a few minutes. He taps on the speaker and remarks, "No problem."

I have used this expression earlier and, as with many of Patrick's phrases, it is difficult knowing whether there is significance or not.

When he begins silly behaviors, I try engaging him in other activities. As we draw, we have a conversation about Patrick "falling apart" and "putting Patrick back together again." After an extended going back and forth with this train of thought, he mentions David Copperfield, the magician he has seen on TV.

"He fall down and lost his head. He fall down and go splash, his head walk away."

This has made a great impression on him. It is difficult to say whether there is a connection with what is going on at the moment, or in his past experience. This session is very calm, and he is compliant and responsive to all that I do with him.

At the next session on Saturday with his mother present, Patrick begins again by acting silly in the mirror as he did when he first came with her. He remembers the *Om-Pa-Pa* song from the Tuesday session on our ride back to school. He can sing on key and with perfect rhythm. As his mother begins to talk, he fiddles with the crayons and makes silly sounds to attract my attention. He even taps me on the leg and begins *Om-Pa-Pa*.

When the dolphin sounds become more chatty, he says, "chickens" and mimics the sounds.

"Do the dolphins sound like chickens?"

"Yes," he responds. (And at that point, they do.)

With the unhooked phone, I try to engage him in a play phone conversation. His mother enters with the suggestion that he learn his phone number. He is resistant to both of our ideas.

"No, no, no! No school allowed."

It is Saturday, and he makes it very clear that anything associated with school, like learning numbers, is not allowed in our session.

"On Tuesday, when we come from school, is it allowed?"

"Yes," agrees Patrick.

It appears that Patrick will be running these sessions his own way! During the remainder of the session he is silly and loud. I wonder if on the days when his mother brings him, we would be better alone.

When I pick Patrick up on the next Tuesday, he is irritable and very quiet on the way over to the session. In the Dolphin Room I try to pacify him with our drawing activity, but he becomes very angry with me when I won't draw a truck. I explain that I don't know how (knowing that *he* does) and ask him to teach me to draw one.

"Be my teacher," I say, "I need a good teacher."

His response is explosive.

"Bad teacher! Leave me alone!"

I quietly suggest that if he wants to be left alone that he ask in a nicer way. We are quiet, listening to the sounds for awhile, and he seems to calm down. I move to the speaker, listening to the sounds and leaving him alone. Soon he begins making noises and kicking things to attract my attention.

"You're not in a very good mood today are you, Patrick?"

"Leave me alone!!!" he screams, rolling over on his stomach, then apologetically, "I'm sorry."

I assure him that it's O.K., saying, "I like you no matter what."

A few minutes go by, and as if to test what I just said, he explodes into a tantrum, flinging things around the room and screaming, "Leave me alone!"

He goes to the amplifier and turns off the sounds. (I wonder how he knows to do this.) I go to him, talking quietly, as he calms himself. I rub his back, a technique used by his classmates in school.

He apologizes, "I'm sorry, Libby. I say bad words. Get the bugs out of my shoulders," as I continue rubbing them. He settles down quickly and is quite upset with himself and his tantrum. He apologizes again and again and is very remorseful. I congratulate him on the way he has pulled himself together. As I say this, I wonder if there is a connection to the "falling to pieces" and "falling apart" phrases he uses frequently.

As we leave, I mention next time. He says, "No next time."

I think he is afraid I won't want him back.

Driving back to school, I turn on my CD and play the theme from *Forrest Gump*. It is an orchestral piece with a piano being played like a music box. It is calm and soothing. He listens quietly, requesting it again and again. When I return him to school, I report his tantrum. The teacher says, "He is not very happy today. His favorite teacher is absent."

Later, when I viewed the tape, I realized the very moment Patrick lost his control was the mention of him being a teacher for me. This set off a chain reaction related to his experience of the day. He couldn't tell me what had gone on in his day, but my use of the word "teacher" was all he needed to react.

How many times are we "normal" people set off by cues we don't recognize, reacting to something that hurt us earlier in our experience. I was learning even more than I expected from these wonderful and unique individuals.

In session four, Patrick is again calm and responsive. His mother says he has not mentioned the tantrum and was excited about coming today. His language is advancing with more fluid sentences and more expression in his voice.

"Libby's a naughty little girl," he teases.

"Poor Libby had a car accident. I put the car back together again."

As we are conversing, he mentions the temper tantrum and follows it with "fall to pieces." Perhaps there is a connection, even in his mind. He apologizes again.

As we drive from school a week after the session in which he had his tantrum, he requests the *Forrest Gump* theme. He is relaxed and compliant but is not as focused today. He uses less self-initiated sentences and more nonsense talk. He is not misbehaving but does not want to participate in our usual activities.

In the sixth session, even though his mother has brought him, I see him alone. He comes in, relaxed, gets a pillow and lies down on the floor. He is quiet and works a puzzle as I draw. When I start to make nonsense sounds, he says, "Idiot Libby" and a few other names. This opens an opportunity to talk about others teasing him and hurting his feelings. He seems to understand as I ask him if others call him names. He answers questions with yes and no only.

As I draw him into a conversation with a cat puppet, his sentences become longer and he becomes very creative. There is quite a bit of hitting of the puppets and "smash to pieces" talk, but overall he is just a boisterous young boy. Some of his phrases are quite humorous as he talks for the toy puppet.

"O.K., no more Mr. Nice Guy. Get a grip, dog."

As the session ends, he says, "How about go turn the power off?"

In session seven, Patrick poses for a "portrait" as I draw. He is quiet and intent on my activity. I ask him questions about what he wants me to draw.

"What kind of mouth do you want: sad, happy, mad?"

"Put an expression."

"What kind of expression?"

Pause.... "Great satisfaction!"

Sometimes I just can't believe what comes out of his mouth.

As he watches, he hums the *Forrest Gump* theme, right on pitch. When I mention *Forrest Gump* he says, "No Gumps allowed." I show him his picture, he looks at it, then at the mirror, then back at the picture.

"Not me," he says, "don't like the expression."

Together we sing the *Forrest Gump* theme on a "Bum, Bum, Bum" syllable and incorporate it into a game with the cat puppet. He has such a wonderful sense of humor and isn't inappropriate with his laughter as we play and giggle together. As the sounds go off, he becomes loud again.

The last session is much as the one before, playful and calm. On Saturdays, before he comes he has watched cartoons, and much of his conversation reflects this influence. It becomes almost a mantra as he obsesses over a phrase. Suddenly, he will come out with a completely original and brilliant observation of his own. He truly is a joy and a puzzle all at the same time, as are all of these gifts I have been loaned by these wonderful parents.

As I review Patrick's tapes, it is impossible to know whether the dolphin sounds made any impression or affect at all. As with the others, he is very sensitive to sounds and is bothered by certain ones. He was not bothered by any of the dolphin sounds. The room certainly seems to have a calming effect, and he and I got along very well throughout. Was it just a coincidence the *Forrest Gump* theme was a defining moment in the time we spent together?

When asked if he wanted me to record the dolphin sounds for home he said, "No, I want *Forrest Gump.*"

His mother told me later that he literally wore out the tape.

What did I learn from Patrick, Robin? What did you observe that I may have missed. I know that he liked me and enjoyed the room, but other than the first time, he paid no attention to the dolphin sounds. In fact, when it came to sounds, it was *Forrest Gump* that touched him more than anything. If he had seen the movie, I might have made a connection, but he had never even heard of it. And what do you make of his nonsense talk? Was it just nonsense, or did it have special meaning to him which only he understood? There was so much beneath the outer silliness of Patrick: his humor, his sensitivity, his poetic soul. How much does he know about his limitations, and how much does it hurt him when he can't communicate his frustrations?

His mother told me in our first interview that his favorite story is Pinnochio; he, too, wants to become "a real boy." Does he know that, inside, he already is?

When it comes to communication, is it not *we* who must understand how *they* communicate and not the other way around? Why should they have to be like us? What are they really trying to say to us about the world we live in and how we live in it as "normal" people?

The questions you ask, Libby Layne, are questions you might ask of anyone, whether or not they have autism, Down's Syndrome, or any so-called disability. Every human is born with a need to communicate. Each has limitations that make communicating with others difficult. Each spends a lifetime learning how to connect with others.

Within each human is a sensitive soul, a poet. There is also the nonsense and silliness, used as defense against hurt and frustration. Remember when you were a little girl...

...I used to get so silly when I knew no other way to get attention. I also used being loud and crazy to hide my hurt or confusion. I mugged in front of the home movie camera to excess and was teased constantly by my family. It hurt my feelings, but weren't they right? I *was* overdoing it; I didn't know why. It has taken me a lifetime of learning to communicate honestly with others about my feelings, without resorting to cover-ups.

What about eye contact? It was not until I was twenty-nine years old that I could look anyone straight in the eye. I had been cross-eyed as a child and always feared they might notice. Even years after my eyes straightened out, I avoided the intensity of eye-contact. I was not aware of this until a director of a children's play I was in called my attention to it.

"You never look me in the eye when I talk to you. Why is that?"

Not until that moment did I become aware that my avoidance was intentional and began my rehabilitation, my retraining to meet others' gaze without fear. It took time and concentration to make myself do it.

Though I have no outward or diagnosed disability, two behaviors that affected my life were behaviors a person with autism might also have.

People with autism have trouble communicating with us; we have trouble communicating with them. They are different, sometimes strange and impossible to understand. For some reason, they go into a world of their own to escape from the noise and confusion of this world. They shut us out and won't let us touch them because it hurts too much.

What I see in Patrick and every other person with whom I work is an exaggeration of what we all face each day in the search to be a "real boy" or a "real girl."

I tried my best to find this real person in Dylan, Kim, James and Patrick. I did the same thing with Pringle. The desire of my heart was to reach that real person inside and communicate love and understanding. Autism is, among other things, a reflection, a reminder, of a major problem on the earth among its creatures. This problem is worst in the human creature.

Somewhere in time, man began concentrating on the differences that exist between him and other creatures, especially other humans. Differences, such as the color of skin, the shape of the eyes, the country of birth, the language one spoke, or the religion one professed, became barriers to communication. Humans began thinking that if others looked, acted or believed differently, they were inferior. This gave them an excuse to treat these humans in an unloving way. In the same way, humans began thinking they were superior to, and separate from, all the rest of creation. Likewise, they became unloving to the earth and its creatures.

When humans separate themselves from each other and the rest of creation, they also separate themselves from the Creator. They forget how to communicate with each other, with other creatures, with creation itself and finally, they forget how to communicate with the Creator.

So where does that leave me now in my quest for Truth? Robin has made me aware of the three gifts I was given for this journey. Haven't they taught me more than I could have ever hoped?

First there is my love of and talent for music. It led me to an understanding of music and its healing power. Throughout all time, music has drawn us closer to our Creator and to Creation itself.

From the most primitive tribe, beating animal skin drums and blowing through reed tubes, to Haydn's *Creation* and Beethoven's *Ode to Joy*, human souls have learned to know God through music. Even the *Forrest Gump* song or *Twinkle, Twinkle Little Star*, played on the piano like a music box, were healing sounds for Patrick and Pringle. But feeling for music is not the common denominator. *Music* is not the "spiritual unified field" for which I have searched, though there is a connection.

There is the gift of my compassion for special children which led me ultimately to individuals with autism. I learned from them how to communicate in new and different ways; there are many kinds of communication. No matter what the barriers, we must learn to care enough about each other to open windows of communication. When we do this, we also renew our communication with the Creator God. Yet communication itself is not Truth with a capital "T", though there is a connection.

As I recall each lesson taught me during my journey, I am grateful for the many truths I have been allowed to discover. Yet, I still feel that there is something I've missed.

Does this mean that I, too, am doomed to give up my quest and say, "There is no Truth with a capital 'T'"?

Is the mystery of the *Sound of the Dolphin's Psalm* to remain a mystery?

Why can't I be satisfied with all I've learned?

I suppose it's that third gift, isn't it Robin? *My Spirit of Tenacity* will not let me off the hook yet!

I shall take just *one* more look!

XIV
Finale

I go to my bookshelf, vaguely remembering something I had read in Tomatis's book *The Conscious Ear.* I turn the page to the chapter called "Sonic Birth." In it, Dr. Tomatis tells of working with a twelve-year-old child who is schizophrenic. Using directional loud speakers, he was experimenting with different artificially produced sound frequencies. I had highlighted the following:

"I simply wanted to make the child listen to filtered sounds that resemble the acoustic impressions the fetus receives in the womb and, in particular, the mother voice, which comes across like a fantastic rustling. I had eliminated all low notes in order to simulate intrauterine hearing. All that remained were the high notes that corresponded to this rustling."

Suddenly I can't sit still! My heart is pounding, my breathing quickens, the pacing begins. There is something extremely important in this! Follow it through!

When I swim with the dolphins, I experience something extraordinary. The magic is not supernatural but *nature* at its *supreme!* I can feel the vibration of the dolphin communications like a sonic massage, soothing both my physical body and my emotions. It is as though every cell in my body is set into a sympathetic vibration with their sounds. On board the boat afterward, these powerful emotions spill over into tears of joy and wonder.

When I return home, I also feel the effects of the dolphin experience. My senses are heightened, and I become unusually creative. Poetry flows, songs are composed, new ideas surface. Is it the sounds or the experience as a whole — the ocean, the sky, the people, the beauty? There is still more, I know it now! "Keep searching," says my Spirit!

I finally settle down and drift off into a reverie of an encounter. The water is warm, clear and barely moving. I cannot feel where my body leaves off and the water begins; we are one with each other. I

233

float, suspended in an aqua world where there is complete peace. I feel no fear as the dolphins circle around me. I am safe in their world. I am accepted totally; I belong here.

I hear not only the sounds the dolphins make but can *feel* them. They become a part of me. Waves of sound are carried on waves of water to my brain, from the fluid that surrounds me through fluid that fills my ears. I hear the sound of my own breathing, inhaling-exhaling, inhaling-exhaling. I hear the sound of my heart beating rhythmically, steady, faithful. I am surrounded by a womb-like environment. It is familiar. I feel safe. I feel secure. I am loved.

From a place deep in my soul, a memory rises. I have lived in this environment before! In it I am suspended in a warm liquid which not only touches every part of my tiny body, but fills my ears. I feel no fear, I am confident in this world, I am accepted totally, I belong here.

The sounds I hear are soothing, calming, comforting. I hear the sound of air being inhaled-exhaled, inhaled-exhaled. I hear the rhythmic beat of my mother's heart, steady, faithful. I hear music, voices, a million other unknown sounds, all filtered through a fluid that has been created solely for my nurturing and development.

And my mother's voice! Oh, the music of it! It is like an incredible melody, rustling in astounding high frequency sound waves. We are in an intimate communication on this wave of sound, my mother and I. We are one with each other. We are one with the Creator. It is heaven, it is Home!

It is like.... the Dolphin Room!

The color of the room is soothing and surrounds the child like a soft blanket. His reflection in the mirror gives the illusion that he is suspended in an aqua environment; his body is enveloped in blue, and it is difficult to discern where his body stops and the blue begins. The lighting is subtle and low, enhancing the mood of tranquility.

Through the speakers, the sound of the ocean is a reminder of the swooshing of the amniotic fluid. Dolphin sounds of infinite wave frequencies are filtered through this fluid medium, recreating the acoustic environment of the child before birth. In this simulated aqua-world, sounds from the outer world are also muffled, hushed, more acceptable to sensitive ears. I recall that every single child in my study responded to numbers seven and eight on the CD. This sequence of dolphin sounds is called "mother-infant bonding." I call it the "chatty section."

The autistic children are reminded of a calmer, safer world, completely opposite from the distorted autistic one in which they find themselves! In the simulated womb-like environment of the Dolphin Room, each individual feels safe enough to open a window. Through this window I am allowed to enter his world and offer my love and encouragement.

I am almost there, my Spirit tells me. There is but one more clue. For this, I must return to the Dolphin Room. I need to experience it again myself.

I enter, setting the light to a dim glow. I turn on the sound system, adjusting the equalizer as I had so many times to tune in the highest possible frequencies. I go to the center of the room, directly between the two speakers. With the remote control in my hand I lie down on the soft plush carpet, looking up at the ceiling where waves of sunlight and water have been beautifully painted. I press the button for number seven on the CD: mother-infant bonding. The speakers come alive. Closing my eyes, I hear the high frequency squeaks and whistles of the dolphins, filtered through the waves of the ocean. I hear the mother dolphin bonding with her infant, their animated chatter filling the room. A smile comes to my lips, then spreads as a warm glow throughout my body as they carry on an intimate communication only *they* can understand. Yet I comprehend its meaning.

The DOLFA-WAVES set up a vibration in the air around me. These vibrations are collected by my outer ear and move to my ear drum which also takes up the vibration. Behind this membrane, three tiny bones join in moving the vibrations inward to minute hairs which excitedly send a message to the seashell-shaped cochlea.

Alerted, the acoustic nerve passes the coded vibrational message to my brain where a memory lies deeply hidden. This unconscious memory has been the force driving my need to communicate, to connect with others from a time before I was born. It is a memory of my first and most intimate experience of communication.

Then slowly the memory begins to awaken. Like the baby dolphin and me in that magical encounter, it rises from the depths, swimming breathlessly through an ocean of time. It accelerates as it nears the light of awareness. Then, in a final burst of energy it breaks the surface of my consciousness in a joyous leap of exhilaration and knowing.

No wonder the children of DOLFA-WAVE communicated with me. No wonder they felt safe in entering my world, in allowing me into theirs. The sound coming through those speakers is nothing less than a simulation of their first experience of their *mother's voice*.

It is the sound of creation!

It is the sound of love!

Oh, Robin Elizabeth, *that's* what the O L stands for, isn't it? DOLFA-WAVE is the sound Of Love. I should have known.

XV
Amen

God By Any Other Name

Sing to the Lord a New Song!
Invoking the many Names of God.
Let us Sing with one Voice, all ye peoples.
In a mighty chorus, let all creatures of the Earth
Join, Praising the One God!
For it is in Praising God Together,
That we shall co-create a New Heaven and A New Earth.

Benissez le Seigneur, Barukh Ata Adonai, Bless the Lord!
Let us find Blessing in feast and in famine,
In Wealth and Poverty,
In Peace and War.
That through the act of Blessing,
There will be no more Famine,
No more Poverty,
No more War.

Creator Spiritus, Brahma, The Word!
Through whom all things came into being,
Help us to see You in Your Creation,
To recognize Your presence in All around us,
And that by acknowledging that presence,
We may understand more of who You are.
For Your creatures show us Your nature in theirs,
The dogs show Your faithfulness and unconditional love,
The oxen, the burdens You will bear,
The dolphins Your grace and playfulness,
And Your peace is cooed by the doves.

Om Padme Hum, Ya-Rahman, Ya-Ghaffar, Ya-Sabir!
Have Compassion on your Children,
Who live in ghettos and roam the street in gangs,
Seeking a family in which to belong.
Have Mercy on Your Children,
Living in fine houses and roaming country clubs,
Who seek, also, a family in which to belong.

Kyrie Eleison, Christe Eleison, Kyrie Eleison!
Forgive us our inability to forgive.
We have become self-centered and self-absorbed.
We place blame and declare ourselves victims,
While the real victims go without help.
We are so intent in searching to "find ourselves,"
We have lost each other and You.

Krishna, Ya-Fattah, Yahweh Elohim!
Enlighten us with Your Spirit.
Teach us that within each of us,
There is a place where You Dwell,
If only we allow You to lead us there.

Eli, Eli, Shiva, Vishnu, Ya-Hafiz!
Preserve and save us from ourselves,
For in our greed and carelessness,
We are destroying our environment.
In our neglect and abuse,
We are destroying our families.
In our hate and prejudice,
We are destroying each other.

Allahu Akhar, Laudate Dominum! Praise God in His Sanctuary.
For the Holy Tabernacle of Adonai,
Is not a place of stone or brick,
It is not a high mountain or a deep valley.
For the Holy Tabernacle, where Ya-Mutkabir dwells,
Is found in the hearts of the people,
Who love and serve each other.
For Buddha, El Shaddai, Yahweh,
Is greater than any Name we can invoke.

Ya-Salaam, Prince of Peace, Jesus Christ,
Teach us to replace the Baseless Hate
That causes ancient rivalries and genocide,
With Baseless Love that knows no bounds.
For until we have peace in our hearts,
There will be no Peace on Earth.
Shalom, Om Shanti, Peace Be with You.

YHWH!
Let us Praise God without Pronoun,
For God is beyond, He, or She,
And honors both the Masculine and the Feminine,

Eck Ong Kar Nam Siri Wha Guru!
O Supreme One, Whose Names are many,
Make us mindful that until we sing together,
The Kingdom will never Come.
Let us Sing a New Song,
Invoking the Greatest Name of all for God,
And that name is LOVE.

BIBLIOGRAPHY

Campbell, Don. *Music, Physician for Times to Come.* Wheaton, Illinois, USA, India, London: Quest Books — The Theosophical Publishing House, 1991

Cameron, Anne. *Daughters of Copper Woman,* Press Gang Publishers, 603 Powell Street, Vancouver, B.C. V6AlH2, 1981

Cochrane, A.& Callen, K. *Dolphins and Their Power To Heal.* Rochester, Vermont: Healing Arts Press, 1992

Dobbs, Horace. *The Magic of Dolphins.* Sheridan House Inc., 145 Palisade St., Dobbs Ferry, New York 10522, 1990

Dobbs, Horace. *Dance to the Dolphin Song.* Jonathan Cape Ltd., 20 Vauxhall Bridge Rd., London, 1991

Fideler, David. *Jesus Christ, Sun of God (Ancient Cosmology and Early Christian Symbolism).* The Theosophical Publishing House, P.O. Box 270, Wheaton, Illinois, 1993

Kaufmann, Barry Neil. *Son Rise, The Miracle Continues.* Tiburon, California: H.J. Kramer, 1979 expanded edition 1993

Merle, Robert. *Day of the Dolphin.* New York: Simon and Schuster, 1969

Rogers, Dale Evans. *Angel Unaware.* Grand Rapids, Michigan: Revell, Fleming H., A division of Baker Book House Co., 1953

Stehli, Annabel. *The Sound of a Miracle,* New York: Doubleday, 1991

Tomatis, Alfred. *The Conscious Ear.* Originally published in French as *L'Oreille et la Vie.* 1977, 1990 Editions. Robert Laffort, S.A., Station Hill Press Inc., Barrytown, New York 12507, and Sound, Listening and Learning Center Inc., 2701 E. Camelback Rd. Suite 205, Phoenix, Arizona 85016, 1991

Williams, Donna. *Nobody, Nowhere.* New York: Times Books, A division of Random House, 1992

Williams, Donna. *Somebody, Somewhere.* New York: Times Books, A division of Random House, 1994

ABOUT THE AUTHOR

Libby Layne has spent the past twenty-eight years researching extensively the fields of music and sound therapy, dolphins and their communications, and children with disabilities, especially autism. She has a Bachelor's Degree in Music Education and a Masters Degree in Counseling. She has taught music in various settings and has worked with many "special" children — those with Down's Syndrome, Attention Deficit Disorder, Pervasive Developmental Disorder, Emotionally Disturbed Teenagers and students with Learning Difficulties, mental retardation, brain damage, and autism.

For the past nine years she has been swimming in the open ocean with wild dolphins.

She lives with her husband in Virginia and has three grown children and three grandchildren. This is her first book.

Libby Layne